GENESIS

Chapters 16—33

J. Vernon McGee

THOMAS NELSON PUBLISHERS

Nashville • Atlanta • London • Vancouver

Copyright © 1991 by Thru the Bible Radio

Published in Nashville, Tennessee, by Thomas Nelson, Inc.

Scripture quotations are from the KING JAMES VERSION of the Bible.

Library of Congress Cataloging-in-Publication Data

McGee, J. Vernon (John Vernon), 1904–1988
    [Thru the Bible with J. Vernon McGee]
    Thru the Bible commentary series / J. Vernon McGee.
        p.   cm.
    Reprint. Originally published: Thru the Bible with J. Vernon
McGee. 1975.
    Includes bibliographical references.
    ISBN 0-7852-1002-4 (TR)
    ISBN 0-7852-1068-7 (NRM)
    1. Bible—Commentaries.   I. Title.
BS491.2.M37   1991
220.7′7—dc20   90–41340
                                                                      CIP

Printed in the United States of America
14 15 16 — 03 02 01 00

CONTENTS

GENESIS—CHAPTERS 16—33

PREFACE

The radio broadcasts of the Thru the Bible Radio five-year program were transcribed, edited, and published first in single-volume paperbacks to accommodate the radio audience.

There has been a minimal amount of further editing for this publication. Therefore, these messages are not the word-for-word recording of the taped messages which went out over the air. The changes were necessary to accommodate a reading audience rather than a listening audience.

These are popular messages, prepared originally for a radio audience. They should not be considered a commentary on the entire Bible in any sense of that term. These messages are devoid of any attempt to present a theological or technical commentary on the Bible. Behind these messages is a great deal of research and study in order to interpret the Bible from a popular rather than from a scholarly (and too-often boring) viewpoint.

We have definitely and deliberately attempted "to put the cookies on the bottom shelf so that the kiddies could get them."

The fact that these messages have been translated into many languages for radio broadcasting and have been received with enthusiasm reveals the need for a simple teaching of the whole Bible for the masses of the world.

I am indebted to many people and to many sources for bringing this volume into existence. I should express my especial thanks to my secretary, Gertrude Cutler, who supervised the editorial work; to Dr. Elliott R. Cole, my associate, who handled all the detailed work with the publishers; and finally, to my wife Ruth for tenaciously encouraging me from the beginning to put my notes and messages into printed form.

Solomon wrote, ". . . of making many books there is no end; and much study is a weariness of the flesh" (Eccl. 12:12). On a sea of books that flood the marketplace, we launch this series of THRU THE BIBLE with the hope that it might draw many to the one Book, *The Bible.*

J. VERNON McGEE

The Book of
GENESIS

INTRODUCTION

The Book of Genesis is one of the two important key books of the Bible. The book that opens the Old Testament (Genesis) and the book that opens the New Testament (Matthew) are the two books which I feel are the key to the understanding of the Scriptures

Before beginning this study, I would like to suggest that you read the Book of Genesis through. It would be preferable to read it at one sitting. I recognize that this may be impossible for you to do, and if you want to know the truth, I have not been able to do it in one sitting. It has taken me several sittings because of interruptions. However, if you find it possible to read through Genesis at one sitting, you will find it very profitable.

Let me give you a bird's-eye view of Genesis, a view that will cover the total spectrum of the book. There are certain things that you should note because the Book of Genesis is, actually, germane to the entire Scripture. The fact of the matter is that Genesis is a book that states many things for the first time: creation, man, woman, sin, sabbath, marriage, family, labor, civilization, culture, murder, sacrifice, races, languages, redemption, and cities.

You will also find certain phrases that occur very frequently. For instance, "these are the generations of" is an important expression used frequently because the Book of Genesis gives the families of early history. That is important to us because we are members of the human family that begins here.

A number of very interesting characters are portrayed for us.

Someone has called this "the book of biographies." There are Abraham, Isaac, Jacob, Joseph, Pharaoh, and the eleven sons of Jacob besides Joseph. You will find that God is continually blessing Abraham, Isaac, Jacob, and Joseph. In addition, those who are associated with them—Lot, Abimelech, Potiphar, the butler, and Pharaoh—are also blessed of God.

In this book you will find mention of the covenant. There are frequent appearances of the Lord to the patriarchs, especially to Abraham. The altar is prominent in this book. Jealousy in the home is found here. Egypt comes before us in this book as it does nowhere else. The judgments upon sin are mentioned here, and there are evident leadings of Providence.

As we study, we need to keep in mind something that Browning wrote years ago in a grammarian's funeral essay: "Image the whole, then execute the parts. Fancy the fabric, quiet, e'er you build, e'er steel strike fire from quartz, e'er mortar dab brick." In other words, get the total picture of this book. I tell students that there are two ways of studying the Bible; one is with the telescope and the other way is with the microscope. At first, you need to get the telescopic view. After that, study it with a microscope.

A great preacher of the past, Robinson of England, has written something which I would like to write indelibly on the minds and hearts of God's people today:

We live in the age of books. They pour out for us from the press in an ever increasing multitude. And we are always reading manuals, textbooks, articles, books of devotion, books of criticism, books about the Bible, books about the Gospels, all are devoured with avidity. But what amount of time and labor do we give to the consideration of the Gospels themselves? We're constantly tempted to imagine that we get good more quickly by reading some modern statement of truth which we find comparatively easy to appropriate because it is presented to us in a shape, and from a standpoint, with which our education, or it may be partly association, has made us familiar. But the good we acquire readily is not that which enters most deeply into our being and becomes an abiding possession. It would be well if we could realize quite simply that nothing worth the having is to be gained without the winning. The great truths of nature are not offered to us in such a form as to make it easy to grasp them. The treasures of grace must be sought with all the skill and energy which are characteristic of the man who is searching for goodly pearls. (Robinson, *The Personal Life of the Clergy*.)

I love that statement because I believe that the Bible itself will speak to our hearts in a way that no other book can do. Therefore we have included the text of Scripture in this study. New translations are appearing in our day; in fact, they are coming from the presses as fast and prolifically as rabbits multiply. However, I will continue to use the Authorized or King James Version. I refuse to substitute the pungency of genius with the bland, colorless, and tasteless mediocrity of the present day.

MAJOR DIVISIONS OF THE BOOK

Where would you divide the Book of Genesis if you divided it into two parts? Notice that the first eleven chapters constitute a whole and that, beginning with chapter 12 through the remainder of the book, we find an altogether different section. The two parts differ in several ways: The first section extends from creation to Abraham. The second section extends from Abraham through Joseph. The first section deals with major *subjects*, subjects which still engage the minds of thoughtful men in our day: the Creation, the Fall, the Flood, the Tower of Babel. The second section has to do with personalities: Abraham, the man of faith; Isaac, the beloved son; Jacob, the chosen and chastened son; and Joseph, his suffering and glory.

Although that is a major division, there is another division even more significant. It has to do with *time*. The first eleven chapters cover a minimum time span of two thousand years—actually, two thousand years plus. I feel that it is safe to say that they may cover several hundred thousand years. I believe this first section of Genesis can cover any time in the past that you may need to fit into your particular theory, and the chances are that you would come short of it even then. At least we know the book covers a minimum of two thousand years in the first eleven chapters, but the second section of thirty-nine chapters covers only three hundred and fifty years. In fact, beginning with Genesis 12 and running all the way through the Old Testament and the New Testament, a total time span of only two thousand years is covered. Therefore, as far as *time* is concerned, you are halfway through the Bible when you cover the first eleven chapters of Genesis.

This should suggest to your mind and heart that God had some definite purpose in giving this first section to us. Do you think that God is putting the emphasis on this first section or on the rest of the Bible? Isn't it evident that He is putting the emphasis on the last part? The first section has to do with the universe and with creation, but the last part deals with man, with nations, and with the person of Jesus Christ. God was more interested in Abraham than He was in the entire created universe. And, my friend, God is more interested in *you* and attaches more value to *you* than He does to the entire physical universe.

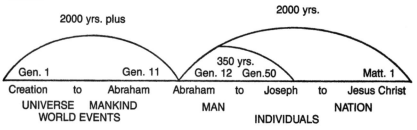

Let me further illustrate this. Of the eighty-nine chapters in the four Gospel records, only four chapters cover the first thirty years of the life of the Lord Jesus while eighty-five chapters cover the last three years of His life, and twenty-seven chapters cover the final eight *days* of His life. Where does that indicate that the Spirit of God is placing the emphasis? I am sure you will agree that the emphasis is on the last part, the last eight days covered by the twenty-seven chapters. And what is that all about? It's about the death, burial, and resurrection of the Lord Jesus Christ. That is the important part of the Gospel record. In other words, God has given the Gospels that you might believe that Christ died for our sins and that He was raised for our justification. That is essential. That is the all-important truth.

May I say that the first eleven chapters of Genesis are merely the introduction to the Bible, and we need to look at them in this fashion. This does not mean that we are going to pass over the first eleven chapters. Actually, we will spend quite a bit of time with them.

Genesis is the "seed plot" of the Bible, and here we find the beginning, the source, the birth of everything. The Book of Genesis is just like the bud of a beautiful rose, and it opens out into the rest of the Bible. The truth here is in germ form.

One of the best divisions which can be made of the Book of Genesis is according to the genealogies—i.e., according to the families.

Gen. 1—2:6	Book of Generations of Heavens and Earth
Gen. 2:7—6:8	Book of Generations of Adam
Gen. 6:9—9:29	Generations of Noah
Gen. 10:1—11:9	Generations of Sons of Noah
Gen. 11:10–26	Generations of Sons of Shem
Gen. 11:27—25:11	Generations of Terah
Gen. 25:12–18	Generations of Ishmael
Gen. 25:19—35:29	Generations of Isaac
Gen. 36:1—37:1	Generations of Esau
Gen. 37:2—50:26	Generations of Jacob

All of these are given to us in the Book of Genesis. It is a book of families. Genesis is an amazing book, and it will help us to look at it from this viewpoint.

OUTLINE

I. **Entrance of Sin on Earth, Chapters 1—11**
   A. Creation, Chapters 1—2
      1. Heaven and Earth, 1:1
         "Create" (bara) occurs only 3 times, vv. 1, 21, 27
      2. Earth Became Waste and Void, 1:2
      3. Re-creation, 1:3—2:25
         (a) First Day—Light, 1:3-5
         (b) Second Day—Air Spaces (Firmament), 1:6-8
         (c) Third Day—
             Dry Land Appears and Plant Life, 1:9-13
         (d) Fourth Day—Sun, Moon, Stars Appear, 1:14-19
         (e) Fifth Day—Animal Life (Biology), 1:20-23
         (f) Sixth Day—
             Fertility of Creation and Creation of Man 1:24-31
         (g) Seventh Day—Sabbath, 2:1-3
         (h) Recapitulation of the Creation of Man, 2:4-25
             (Law of recurrence)

   B. Fall, Chapters 3—4
      1. Root of Sin—Doubting and Disobeying God
      2. Fruit of Sin—
         "Out of the heart proceed . . . murders . . ."
         (Matt. 15:19)

   C. Flood (Deluge), Chapters 5—9
      1. Book of Generations of Adam—Through Seth
         Beginning of Man's History—
         Obituary Notices, Chapter 5
      2. Antediluvian Civilization—
         Cause of Flood and Construction of Ark, Chapter 6
      3. Judgment of Flood, Chapter 7
      4. Postdiluvian Civilization—
         After the Flood, Chapter 8

CHAPTER 16

THEME· Sarai's suggestion; Hagar flees; the tests of Abraham

As we come to this chapter, I must confess that I almost wish it were not in the Bible. After Abram rose to the heights in chapter 15, you would say that he certainly is treading on high places—but he is not perfect. In chapter 16 we see the lapse of this man's faith relative to Sarai and Hagar, the Egyptian maid. We have here the unbelief of both Sarai and Abram, and the birth of Ishmael. This is certainly a letdown after the wonder of the previous chapter.

SARAI'S SUGGESTION

Now Sarai Abram's wife bare him no children: and she had an handmaid, an Egyptian, whose name was Hagar [Gen. 16:1].

Abram got two things down in the land of Egypt which really caused him trouble: one was wealth, and the other was this little Egyptian maid.

And Sarai said unto Abram, Behold now, the LORD hath restrained me from bearing: I pray thee, go in unto my maid; it may be that I may obtain children by her. And Abram hearkened to the voice of Sarai [Gen. 16:2].

The thing that Sarai suggested was the common practice of that day. When a wife could not bear a child, there was the concubine. Now don't say that God approved it God did not approve of this at all. This was Sarai's idea, and Abram listened to her. It looks like he is surrendering his position as head of the home here, and he followed her suggestion

> **And Sarai Abram's wife took Hagar her maid the Egyptian, after Abram had dwelt ten years in the land of Canaan, and gave her to her husband Abram to be his wife [Gen. 16:3].**

This little Egyptian maid becomes a concubine, and this is not according to God's will. God is not going to accept the offspring at all— He didn't; He wouldn't. Why? Because it was *wrong*. Don't say that God approved this. All you can say is that this is in the record because it is an historical fact.

> **And he went in unto Hagar, and she conceived: and when she saw that she had conceived, her mistress was despised in her eyes [Gen. 16:4].**

Hagar said, "I've mothered a child of Abram, and Sarai couldn't do it." She looked down on Sarai, you see.

> **And Sarai said unto Abram, My wrong be upon thee: I have given my maid into thy bosom; and when she saw that she had conceived, I was despised in her eyes: the Lord judge between me and thee [Gen. 16:5].**

Don't pass this verse by. Don't assume that God approved of this. God says that it is wrong, and now Sarai sees that she has done wrong. "My wrong be upon thee"—she is *wrong*, my friend. God will not accept this, and it is going to be a real heartbreak to old Abram. But, you see, Abram and Sarai are not really trusting God as they should. After all, Abram at this time is nearly ninety years old and Sarai eighty. I think they have come to the conclusion that they are not going to have a child. Sarai could probably rationalize and say, "I think maybe this is the way God wants us to do it, for this is the custom of the day." It *was* the custom of that day, but it was contrary to God's way of doing things. We get the wrong impression if we think that just because something is recorded in the Bible God approves of it. The

Bible is inspired in that it is an accurate record, but there are many things God does not approve of that are recorded in His Word.

The moral implications that you and I read into this are not quite here in the historical record. Abram and Sarai were brought up in Ur of the Chaldees where this was a common practice, and the moral angle is not the thing that for them was so wrong. The terrible thing was that they just did not believe God. The wrong that they committed by Abram taking Sarai's maid Hagar was a sin, and God treated it as such. But today we reverse the emphasis and say that taking a concubine is a sin, but we do not pay too much attention to the unbelief. Yet the unbelief was the major sin here; that is, it was lots blacker than the other.

HAGAR FLEES

But Abram said unto Sarai, Behold, thy maid is in thy hand; do to her as it pleaseth thee. And when Sarai dealt hardly with her, she fled from her face [Gen. 16:6].

Hagar took off—she ran away—and this would probably have meant death to her and certainly to the child she was carrying.

And the angel of the LORD found her by a fountain of water in the wilderness, by the fountain in the way to Shur [Gen. 16:7].

I am inclined to believe that the Angel of the Lord is none other than the preincarnate Christ. This is characteristic of Him: He is always out looking for the lost. Hagar had traveled quite a distance from home.

And he said, Hagar, Sarai's maid, whence camest thou? and whither wilt thou go? And she said, I flee from the face of my mistress Sarai.

And the angel of the LORD said unto her, Return to thy mistress, and submit thyself under her hands.

> And the angel of the LORD said unto her, I will multiply
> thy seed exceedingly, that it shall not be numbered for
> multitude [Gen. 16:8–10].

In the fourth chapter of the Epistle to the Galatians, Paul uses this as an allegory. He speaks there of Hagar and her offspring as being Mount Sinai where the Mosaic law was given, and he speaks of the legality and the bondage of that law. Then he speaks of Sarai as being the one who is free. The point is that the one who belonged to Abram was Sarai—she was his wife. Many people today want to take on something different; they want to get under the law. But, my friend, as believers we have been joined to Christ. The church has been espoused to Christ, Paul says, as a chaste virgin and will someday be the bride of Christ. Therefore may I say to you, you do not want to take on the law. The law is another one that you and I just don't need; it is like Hagar, and that is the point that Paul is making in Galatians.

This is going to be a great sorrow, not only to Sarai (it already has been to her), but it is going to be an even greater sorrow to Abram later on. Hagar now comes back to give birth to a boy, that boy who happens to be Abram's son.

> And the angel of the LORD said unto her, Behold, thou art
> with child, and shalt bear a son, and shalt call his name
> Ishmael; because the LORD hath heard thy affliction.
>
> And he will be a wild man; his hand will be against
> every man, and every man's hand against him; and he
> shall dwell in the presence of all his brethren [Gen.
> 16:11–12].

Have you looked at this verse in light of about four thousand years of history in the Middle East? What is going on out there today? The descendants of Ishmael are wild men—that has been the story of those Bedouin tribes of the desert down through the centuries, and it is a fulfillment of the prophecy that God gave. They will tell you that they are sons of Abraham, but they are also sons of Ishmael. They are related to Abraham through Ishmael.

> And she called the name of the LORD that spake unto her,
> Thou God seest me: for she said, Have I also here looked
> after him that seeth me?

> Wherefore the well was called Beerlahairoi; behold, it is
> between Kadesh and Bered [Gen. 16:13–14].

How gracious God is to Hagar! It is not her sin, so God very graciously deals with her. Let me repeat that I believe the Angel of the Lord here is none other than the preincarnate Christ gone out to seek the lost again. He's that kind of Shepherd, and He brings to her this good word.

"And she called the name of the LORD that spake unto her, Thou God seest me." This is something new to her that she did not realize before. The Egyptians did have a very primitive idea and conception of God. "For she said, Have I also here looked after him that seeth me?" She is overwhelmed by the fact that she is seen of God. That doesn't seem to be very impressive to us today because we have a higher view of God than that. But wait just a minute! We probably come just as far short of really knowing about God as Hagar did. It is difficult for a little, finite man to conceive of the infinite God, and all of us come short of understanding and of knowing Him. I think that a theme which will engage us throughout the endless ages of eternity is just coming to know God. That is worthy of any man's study. To come to know God is something that will dignify a man's position throughout eternity.

> And Hagar bare Abram a son: and Abram called his
> son's name, which Hagar bare, Ishmael.

> And Abram was fourscore and six years old, when Hagar bare Ishmael to Abram [Gen. 16:15–16].

Remember that Ishmael was Abram's son. Abram was now eighty-six years old.

THE TESTS OF ABRAHAM

Before we go farther, I would like to make a recapitulation of the seven appearances of God to Abram, five of which we have already seen. There were certain failures in the life of Abram, but also there were successes. Actually, there were seven tests which God gave to him:

(1) God called Abram out of Ur of the Chaldees, his home, and Abram responded partially. His faith was weak and imperfect, but at least he moved out. Abram finally arrived safely in the land of Canaan, and God blessed him.

(2) Then there was a famine in the land of Canaan, and Abram fled from the land of Canaan to Egypt. There he acquired riches and Hagar—and both were stumbling blocks.

(3) Abram was given riches which are a real test. They have been a stumbling block to many a man, by the way. Frankly, I have always wished that the Lord would have let me have that kind of test rather than some of the others I've had! But nevertheless, I'm of the opinion that He could not have trusted me with riches. Abram did not forget God, and he was certainly generous and magnanimous toward his nephew Lot. Riches resulted in his separation from Lot, and God appeared to him again.

(4) Abram was given power through his defeat of the kings of the east. That was a real test, for he happened to be the conqueror. This man Melchizedek met him, which I think strengthened Abram for the test, and so he refused the spoils of war. Afterwards, God appeared to Abram and encouraged him.

(5) God delayed giving Abram a son by his wife Sarai. Abram became impatient, and through the prompting of Sarai, he took matters into his own hands and moved outside the will of God. As a result, there was the birth of Ishmael. The Arabs of the desert today still plague the nation Israel, and they will keep right on doing that, I think, until the Millennium

Abraham's two final tests occur (6) at the destruction of Sodom and Gomorrah in chapter 18 and (7) at the offering of his son Isaac in chapter 22.

CHAPTER 17

THEME: God gives Abraham a new name; God's covenant; Ishmael's inheritance

A great many people feel that the seventeenth chapter is the most outstanding chapter of the Book of Genesis. Here God makes a covenant with Abram and confirms His promise to him about a son. He lets Abram know that Ishmael is not the one He promised to him. In one sense this chapter is the key to the Book of Genesis, and it may be a key to the entire Bible. God's covenant with Abram concerns two important items: a seed and a land. He reveals Himself to Abram by a new name—*El Shaddai,* the Almighty God—and He also gives Abram a new name. Up to this point his name was Abram; now it is changed to Abraham. *Abram* means "high father," and *Abraham* means "father of a multitude." That Ishmael was not the son God promised to Abraham is the thing this chapter makes very clear.

GOD GIVES ABRAHAM A NEW NAME

And when Abram was ninety years old and nine, the LORD appeared to Abram, and said unto him, I am the Almighty God; walk before me, and be thou perfect [Gen. 17:1].

Think of that! Abram was eighty-six years old when Ishmael was born, and it was not until fourteen years later that Isaac was born.

"The LORD appeared to Abram, and said unto him, I am the Almighty God; walk before me, and be thou perfect." God says, "I am *El Shaddai,* the Almighty God"—this is a new name.

And I will make my covenant between me and thee, and will multiply thee exceedingly [Gen. 17:2].

Thirteen times in this chapter we find the word *covenant*. For it to appear thirteen times in twenty-seven verses obviously means that God is talking about the covenant. This is God's fifth appearance to Abram. He comes now not only to make the covenant, but also to reaffirm the promise of a son that He has made, which absolutely rules out this boy Ishmael, of course.

Paul, writing in the fourth chapter of Romans, says this: "And being not weak in faith, he considered not his own body now dead, when he was about an hundred years old, neither yet the deadness of Sarah's womb" (Rom. 4:19).

Sarah's womb actually was a tomb—it was the place of death. And out of death came life: Isaac was born. Paul concludes that fourth chapter by saying this about the Lord Jesus: "Who was delivered for our offences, and was raised again for our justification" (Rom. 4:25). Life out of death—that is the promise God is now making to this man. Abram is 99 years old, and that means that Sarai is 89 years old. When Isaac was born, Abraham was 100 years old and Sarah 90.

> **And Abram fell on his face: and God talked with him, saying,**
>
> **As for me, behold, my covenant is with thee, and thou shalt be a father of many nations [Gen. 17:3–4].**

God says to Abram that he will be a father of many nations. I suppose it could be said that this man has probably had more children than any other man that has ever lived on the earth, as far as we know. Just think of it: for four thousand years, there have been two great lines— the line of Ishmael and the line of Isaac—and there have been millions in each line. What a family! What a homecoming! Added to that, there is a spiritual seed, for we Christians are called the children of Abraham by faith in Christ. In Romans 4:16, speaking of Abraham, Paul says, ". . . who is the father of us all"—that is, of believers, of the nation Israel, and also of the Arabs, by the way. Just think of the millions of people! God says here, "I am going to make you a father of many nations," and He has made that promise good.

Neither shall thy name any more be called Abram, but thy name shall be Abraham; for a father of many nations have I made thee [Gen. 17:5].

Abram means "high father" or "father of the height" or "exalted father." *Abraham* means "father of a multitude."

I am going to inject a little story here to illustrate to you something of the faith of this man Abram. Suppose that one morning Abram and Sarai get up, and as they are working around the tent there suddenly appears a group of traders at their little oasis created by the spring at Hebron. Abram goes out to meet them, and they want to know if they can water their camels.

There were many hospitable people in that day, and that is quite interesting. We speak of the caveman way back yonder and how terrible he was. May I say to you, in that day a stranger could not go through the country without somebody opening his home and entertaining him. But if you came into Los Angeles as a stranger, I don't know anybody who would take you in, although there are a lot of Christians in this area. Our culture is altogether different today, and we certainly lack the hospitality they had in that day.

Abram goes out to meet them, and the conversation probably sounded like this: "Sure, help yourselves, and I'll feed your stock. Would you like to stay for awhile?" They say, "No, we're on a business trip and are in a hurry to get down to Egypt."

One of the men then says, "My name is Allah," and the other says, "My name is Ali Baba. What's your name?" When Abram replies, "My name is High Father," the men exclaim, "My! Boy or girl?" Abram says, "I don't have any children." The men just laugh and say, "You mean to tell us that you don't have any children and your name is Abram? How in the world can you be a father and not have children?" And they ride off across the desert, laughing.

Six months later, they come by again. When he goes out to greet them again, they all begin to laugh, "Hello there, High Father!" But he says, "My name is not High Father anymore. It is now Father of a Multitude." The traders say, "My, must have been twins!" And then they really laugh when Abraham says, "No, I still don't have any children." They say, "How ridiculous can that be?"

Here was a man who was a father before he had any children. Abraham was Abraham, father of a multitude, by faith at that time. But four thousand years later, where you and I sit, we can say that God sure made this good. The name stuck, if you please, and he is still Abraham, the father of a multitude.

GOD'S COVENANT

And I will make thee exceeding fruitful, and I will make nations of thee, and kings shall come out of thee.

And I will establish my covenant between me and thee and thy seed after thee in their generations for an everlasting covenant, to be a God unto thee, and to thy seed after thee [Gen. 17:6–7].

What kind of covenant did God make with Abraham? An *everlasting* covenant. If it is everlasting, is it good today? It certainly is. God promised you and me everlasting life if we will trust Christ—that is a covenant God has made. My friend, if God is not going to make good this covenant that He made with Abraham, you had better look into yours again. But I have news for you: He is going to make your covenant good, and He is also going to make Abraham's good.

And I will give unto thee, and to thy seed after thee, the land wherein thou art a stranger, all the land of Canaan, for an everlasting possession; and I will be their God [Gen. 17:8].

God tells Abraham what *He* will do. God says, *"I will."* "I will make thee exceeding fruitful, and I will make nations of thee. . . . And I will establish my covenant between me and thee and thy seed. . . . And I will give unto thee, and to thy seed after thee . . . all the land of Canaan, for an everlasting possession."

God has made a covenant with these people that is an everlasting covenant. Since it is, it is not one that will be easily broken, and it is not one that is going to run out. God did not give them a ninety-nine-year lease on the land. God gave them an *everlasting* possession.

The Hebrew people have been in that land on three occasions, and it is theirs, but the important thing is that they occupy it only under certain conditions. First of all, God sent them down into the land of Egypt, and they were dispersed there. They went down a family of about seventy and came out a nation of at least one and one-half million. They were put out of their land again at the Babylonian captivity because they went into idolatry and were not witnessing for God. We find that they again went out of the land in A.D. 70 after they had rejected their Messiah. Actually, they have never been back. God predicted that three times they would be put out of the land and three times they would be returned. They have been returned twice. (I do not consider the present return to the land a fulfillment.) When they return the next time, I take it that it means they will never go out of the land again. The Millennium will take place when God gathers and brings them back into the land.

And God said unto Abraham, Thou shalt keep my covenant therefore, thou, and thy seed after thee in their generations.

This is my covenant, which ye shall keep, between me and thy seed after thee; Every man child among you shall be circumcised.

And ye shall circumcise the flesh of your foreskin; and it shall be a token of the covenant betwixt me and you [Gen. 17:9–11].

Circumcision is the *badge* of the covenant. The Israelites did not circumcise themselves in order to become members of the covenant.

They did this because they *had* the covenant from God. Circumcision occupied the same place that good works occupy for the believer today. You do not perform good works in order to be saved; you perform good works because you *have been* saved. That makes all the difference in the world.

When I went away from home as a boy, although I did get into a lot of trouble, the one thing that kept me from becoming an absolute renegade was the thought of my dad. I said to myself, "Because I'm a son of my father, I won't do this or enter into that." I refrained from things because of my dad. Now, I did not become his son because I did not do certain things. I already was his son. But because I was his son, I didn't do them. The badge of the covenant was circumcision. The thing that put them under the covenant wasn't circumcision, but circumcision was the badge of it, the evidence of it.

And he that is eight days old shall be circumcised among you, every man child in your generations, he that is born in the house, or bought with money of any stranger, which is not of thy seed [Gen. 17:12].

Have you noticed how meticulous the record concerning the birth of Christ is? All the law was fulfilled in connection with the birth of this little baby. It is recorded that He was the son of Abraham, the son of David; He was in the line, and on the eighth day He was circumcised. He was "born under the law," Paul says in Galatians 4:4.

He that is born in thy house, and he that is bought with thy money, must needs be circumcised: and my covenant shall be in your flesh for an everlasting covenant [Gen. 17:13].

Again, circumcision is the badge of the covenant. They did not have to do this in order to get the covenant; God had already made the covenant with them. I trust that you see this because it is so important. The same thing is true today. A great many people think that, if they join the church or are baptized, they will be saved. No, my friend, you don't do those things to get saved. If you are saved, I think you will do both of them—you'll join a church, and you'll be baptized—but you don't do that to get saved. We need to keep the cart where it belongs, following the horse, and not get the cart before the horse. For in fact, in the thinking of many relative to salvation, the horse is in the cart today.

And the uncircumcised man child whose flesh of his foreskin is not circumcised, that soul shall be cut off from his people; he hath broken my covenant [Gen. 17:14].

The fact that there were those who disobeyed (practically the entire nation disobeyed when they came out of the land of Egypt) did not militate against the covenant. That disobedience simply meant that the individual would be put out. However, as far as the nation is concerned, no individual or group could destroy this covenant which God had made with Abraham and his seed after him. It is an everlasting covenant. The man who had broken the covenant was put out, but the covenant stood. That is how marvelous it is.

And God said unto Abraham, As for Sarai thy wife, thou shalt not call her name Sarai, but Sarah shall her name be [Gen. 17:15].

Her name was Sarai before; now it is changed to Sarah.

And I will bless her, and give thee a son also of her: yea, I will bless her, and she shall be a mother of nations; kings of people shall be of her [Gen. 17:16].

If old Abraham is going to be a father of nations, then Sarah is going to be a mother of nations.

Then Abraham fell upon his face, and laughed, and said in his heart, Shall a child be born unto him that is an hundred years old? and shall Sarah, that is ninety years old, bear? [Gen. 17:17].

Old Abraham just laughed. This is not the laughter of unbelief. I think it is the laughter of just sheer joy that this could happen. I am sure that you have had this experience. Every now and then in our lives, God does something for us that is so wonderful that we just feel like laughing. You don't know anything else to do but to laugh about it. This was something unheard of. There was "the deadness of Sarah's womb," and Abraham was "dead"—have you ever noticed how Paul described this? "(As it is written, I have made thee a father of many nations,) before him whom he believed, even God, who quickeneth the dead, and calleth those things which be not as though they were. Who against hope believed in hope, that he might become the father of many nations, according to that which was spoken, So shall thy seed be. And being not weak in faith, he considered not his own body was now dead, when he was about an hundred years old, neither yet the deadness of Sarah's womb: He staggered not at the promise of God through unbelief; but was strong in faith, giving glory to God; And being fully persuaded that, what he had promised, he was able also to perform. And therefore it was imputed to him for righteousness" (Rom. 4:17–22). Abraham believed in God, and he is absolutely overwhelmed by the wonder and the goodness of God.

But then, all of a sudden, a thought comes to Abraham like an arrow to his heart. He thinks of a little boy who is his, a boy by the name of Ishmael.

And Abraham said unto God, O that Ishmael might live before thee! [Gen. 17:18].

Abraham is saying, "Oh, Lord, this little fellow who has been growing up in my home . . . !" Abraham is attached to Ishmael. He was fourteen years old when Abraham sent him out a little later on. I do not think that Abraham ever saw him again. My friend, I don't care what you might think of Ishmael; he was Abraham's son, and Abraham loved his son. It was a heartbreak for him to have to give him up.

I am of the opinion that Abraham thought many, many times, "I made a great big mistake in taking Hagar." You see, that was a sin that not only plagued him, but there has also been trouble in that land from the beginning because Abraham sinned. Don't tell me that sin is a little thing or that sin is something you get by with. "Be not deceived; God is not mocked: for whatsoever a man soweth, that shall he also reap" (Gal. 6:7). A man does not reap something similar; he reaps just that which he sowed. And this man Abraham is certainly reaping: "O that Ishmael might live before thee!"

> And God said, Sarah thy wife shall bear thee a son indeed; and thou shalt call his name Isaac: and I will establish my covenant with him for an everlasting covenant, and with his seed after him [Gen. 17:19].

In other words, God says, "No, I won't accept Ishmael. That was wrong." Don't say that God approved polygamy just because it is recorded in the Bible. I cannot see that He is approving it at all.

ISHMAEL'S INHERITANCE

> And as for Ishmael, I have heard thee: Behold, I have blessed him, and will make him fruitful, and will multiply him exceedingly; twelve princes shall he beget, and I will make him a great nation.

> But my covenant will I establish with Isaac, which Sarah shall bear unto thee at this set time in the next year [Gen. 17:20–21].

God holds to the promise that He has made. God is not to be deterred or deferred from this at all. He is going to do the exact thing that He said He would do. He speaks as if Isaac were already born and in their midst. He speaks of things that are not as if they are—and it *is* going to be next year.

And he left off talking with him, and God went up from Abraham [Gen. 17:22].

In other words, Abraham, you might just as well keep quiet. God has already decided this. My friend, there are things which you and I might as well stop petitioning the Lord for. There are times when you've said enough and you don't need to say any more. Sometimes folk just pester the Lord in a prayer when they already have the answer—which, of course, is *No!* God says to Abraham, "Let this alone, now. This is enough; you need not mention this anymore. I have not accepted it, and I do not intend to." God is going to hear and answer other prayers of Abraham. We will find that God listens to Abraham. However, in the case of His covenant, He is making it with Isaac not with Ishmael. That is settled, and Abraham might just as well stop trying to change God's mind. A great many people today pray about things that God maybe does not intend to hear or answer at all. I try to be very careful about asking people to pray about certain things. I want at least to feel like there is a reasonable chance of God's hearing it and answering.

And Abraham took Ishmael his son, and all that were born in his house, and all that were bought with his money, every male among the men of Abraham's house; and circumcised the flesh of their foreskin in the self-same day, as God had said unto him.

And Abraham was ninety years old and nine, when he was circumcised in the flesh of his foreskin.

And Ishmael his son was thirteen years old, when he was circumcised in the flesh of his foreskin.

In the selfsame day was Abraham circumcised, and Ishmael his son.

And all the men of his house, born in the house, and bought with money of the stranger, were circumcised with him [Gen. 17:23–27].

Circumcision is the badge of the covenant which God has made with Abraham. Someone will ask, "Why was Ishmael included?" Hasn't God promised that Ishmael is going to be a great nation also? He is included in it in that sense, but he is not the one whom God had promised to Abraham at the beginning. He is not to be the father of the nation that God will use and the nation through which the Messiah will come.

CHAPTER 18

THEME: God reaffirms His promise; God announces the coming destruction of Sodom and Gomorrah

Until you get to the New Testament, you may wonder why the eighteenth and nineteenth chapters of Genesis are included in the Bible. They seem rather detached from the story of Abraham. They deal with the destruction of Sodom and Gomorrah.

Chapter 18 is a rather lengthy chapter in which God tells Abraham about the judgment of Sodom and Gomorrah and Abraham intercedes on behalf of the cities of the plain. This is an illustration, I think, of the *blessed* Christian life, of life in fellowship with God. But in chapter 19, down in Sodom and Gomorrah with Lot, we will see what I would call the *blasted* life—all because of a decision that was made.

Unfortunately, we have both kinds among Christians today—those living a blessed life and those living a blasted life. There are those who have really made shipwreck of their lives; they have gotten entirely out of the will of God. I would not suggest even for a moment that they have lost their salvation, but they sure have lost everything else. As Paul says, they are saved, ". . . yet so as by fire"(1 Cor. 3:15).

GOD REAFFIRMS HIS PROMISE

And the LORD appeared unto him in the plains of Mamre: and he sat in the tent door in the heat of the day [Gen. 18:1].

Abraham is living down there in Mamre, and he's an old man, by the way.

And he lift up his eyes and looked, and, lo, three men stood by him: and when he saw them, he ran to meet

them from the tent door, and bowed himself toward the ground [Gen. 18:2].

Notice the hospitality that Abraham extends. The little story that I told in the previous chapter has a basis of fact, at least, although I don't think it ever took place. The point is that this man Abraham is a very gracious, hospitable man.

And said, My Lord, if now I have found favour in thy sight, pass not away, I pray thee, from thy servant:

Let a little water, I pray you, be fetched, and wash your feet, and rest yourselves under the tree [Gen. 18:3–4].

It seems very strange to us to tell a visiting stranger to wash his feet and come in. We wouldn't quite say that today, but this is probably the oldest custom that is known. Remember that in the Upper Room our Lord washed the disciples' feet—and there is a tremendous spiritual message there. Here Abraham says, "Wash your feet." It was a token of real hospitality when someone came into a home to have him take off his shoes and wash his feet. In that day they did not take off their hat, but they did take off their shoes. Today we have reversed it. When you come to visit somebody, you leaves your shoes on and take off your hat. I'm not sure which is right. I like the idea, myself, of taking off my shoes. I like to go barefooted in the summertime. I wish it were possible more often. When I am out in the Hawaiian Islands, I put my shoes away and wear thongs or go barefooted as much as possible. I don't put my shoes back on the whole time I am there. I love to go barefooted. I think this was a great custom. It sure would make you feel at home to take off your shoes, wash your feet, and rest yourself under the shade of a tree. Abraham is really entertaining these men royally.

And I will fetch a morsel of bread, and comfort ye your hearts; after that ye shall pass on: for therefore are ye come to your servant. And they said, So do, as thou hast said.

> And Abraham hastened into the tent unto Sarah, and
> said, Make ready quickly three measures of fine meal,
> knead it, and make cakes upon the hearth.
>
> And Abraham ran unto the herd, and fetched a calf ten-
> der and good, and gave it unto a young man; and he
> hasted to dress it.
>
> And he took butter, and milk, and the calf which he had
> dressed, and set it before them; and he stood by them
> under the tree, and they did eat [Gen. 18:5–8].

Isn't this a marvelous way of entertaining? Abraham has prepared a sumptuous meal. He took a little calf, a servant killed and prepared it, and the chef probably barbecued it. They had veal steaks or veal roast, I imagine, and all the trimmings that went with it. "And he took but-ter, and milk"—my, it was a real feast! Abraham entertains these three guests.

Then we find that these guests are royal guests. In the New Testa-ment it is suggested to us that ". . . some have entertained angels un-awares" (Heb. 13:2). That was Abraham—he didn't know whom he was really entertaining.

> And they said unto him, Where is Sarah thy wife? And
> he said, Behold, in the tent [Gen. 18:9].

It was not proper in that day—and even in the East today—for the wife to come out and be the one to entertain, especially since there were three male guests there. But now they ask and make inquiry about Sarah.

> And he said, I will certainly return unto thee according
> to the time of life; and, lo, Sarah thy wife shall have a
> son. And Sarah heard it in the tent door, which was be-
> hind him [Gen. 18:10].

I think Sarah had her ear to the keyhole and had been listening in. Both Abraham and Sarah now discover that they are entertaining angels unaware.

> **Now Abraham and Sarah were old and well stricken in age; and it ceased to be with Sarah after the manner of women.**
>
> **Therefore Sarah laughed within herself, saying, After I am waxed old shall I have pleasure, my lord being old also? [Gen. 18:11–12].**

That is, Sarah asks, "Is it possible that I will have a son?"—and she laughs. Now what kind of laughter is this? I think this is the laughter which says that it is just too good to be true—that's all. Again, I'm sure that most of us have had experiences like this. God has been so good to us on a certain occasion that we just laughed. Something happened that was just too good to be true, and that was the way Sarah laughed. She is saying, "This is something just too good to be true. It just *can't* happen to me!"

> **And the LORD said unto Abraham, Wherefore did Sarah laugh, saying, Shall I of a surety bear a child, which am old?**
>
> **Is any thing too hard for the LORD? At the time appointed I will return unto thee, according to the time of life, and Sarah shall have a son.**
>
> **Then Sarah denied, saying, I laughed not; for she was afraid. And he said, Nay; but thou didst laugh [Gen. 18:13–15].**

Sarah is frightened by the Lord's question and is certainly rather evasive. but she cannot avoid the truth.

And the men rose up from thence, and looked toward Sodom: and Abraham went with them to bring them on the way [Gen. 18:16].

Abraham didn't have a front gate, so he walked out with them a little farther than the front gate to bid them good-bye. And as they walked out from where Abraham lived, they could look down to Sodom and Gomorrah. When I was in that land, it was amazing to me how far you could see on a clear day. I could see from Jerusalem to Bethlehem. And from the ruins of old Samaria, I could see Jerusalem, the Mediterranean Sea, and the Sea of Galilee. I could see Mt. Hermon from most anyplace—it's tremendous. Abraham walked out a ways with these guests, and down below there, they saw Sodom and Gomorrah. They were the great resorts of that day, and they must have been very delightful and beautiful places to be.

GOD ANNOUNCES THE COMING DESTRUCTION OF SODOM AND GOMORRAH

And the LORD said, Shall I hide from Abraham that thing which I do [Gen. 18:17].

Up to this point, the Lord has not revealed to Abraham what He is going to do with Sodom and Gomorrah: He is going to destroy them. "Shall I hide from Abraham that thing which I do?"

Notice now the reason that God is *not* going to hide it from Abraham.

Seeing that Abraham shall surely become a great and mighty nation, and all the nations of the earth shall be blessed in him? [Gen. 18:18].

Abraham is going to have a tremendous influence. He is going to influence multitudes of people, including the succeeding generations.

That is true right now today. As I write and as you read this book, Abraham is influencing us—we cannot avoid it

> **For I know him, that he will command his children and his household after him, and they shall keep the way of the LORD, to do justice and judgment; that the LORD may bring upon Abraham that which he hath spoken of him [Gen. 18:19].**

God says, "I'd better not hide it from Abraham because he will get a wrong impression of Me." Notice by the way, that this man Abraham had discipline in his household.

> **And the LORD said, Because the cry of Sodom and Gomorrah is great, and because their sin is very grievous;**
>
> **I will go down now, and see whether they have done altogether according to the cry of it, which is come unto me; and if not, I will know [Gen. 18:20–21].**

In other words, God is saying to Abraham, "I know the situation there, but I'm going down to investigate." God never does anything hurriedly or hastily. It is a good thing that God told Abraham He was going to destroy these cities, because otherwise Abraham would have gotten a wrong impression of God. He would have thought that God was rather dictatorial and vindictive and that He was One who apparently showed no mercy for or consideration of those who were His. Abraham would really have had a distorted and warped view of God, and so God lets him know what He is going to do. Abraham now has time to turn this over in his mind. It is also a good thing that God told him because he did have a wrong idea of God and of Sodom and Gomorrah—he was wrong about many things. This is one of the reasons that God is telling us as much as He is. There are a lot of things that He does not tell us, but He has told us enough so that though a man be a fool and a wayfaring man, he needn't err therein.

> And the men turned their faces from thence, and went
> toward Sodom: but Abraham stood yet before the Lord
> [Gen. 18:22].

Abraham is now waiting before the Lord.

> And Abraham drew near, and said, Wilt thou also de-
> stroy the righteous with the wicked? [Gen. 18:23].

What is the first thing that enters Abraham's mind? The first thing
that enters his mind, of course, is Lot. He had rescued Lot once, and
now Lot is again in danger down there. I think that Abraham had wondered many times about Lot and his relationship to God, but at least
he believes that Lot is a saved man. He is asking God, "What about the
righteous?" I believe that Abraham would have told you that he
thought there were many people in the city of Sodom who were saved.
He could not understand why God would destroy the righteous with
the wicked. What a picture we have here!

> Peradventure there be fifty righteous within the city:
> wilt thou also destroy and not spare the place for the
> fifty righteous that are therein? [Gen. 18:24].

Abraham begins with fifty. He says to the Lord, "Lord, suppose there
are fifty righteous down there in Sodom. Would You destroy the city if
there were fifty righteous?"

> That be far from thee to do after this manner, to slay the
> righteous with the wicked: and that the righteous
> should be as the wicked, that be far from thee: Shall not
> the Judge of all the earth do right? [Gen. 18:25].

That is still a question that many people ask: "Shall not the Judge of
all the earth do right?" And there is an answer to it. The rest of the
Bible testifies to the fact that the Judge of all the earth *always* does

right. Whatever God does is right, and if you don't think He is right, the trouble is not with God, but the trouble is with you and your thinking. You are thinking wrong; you do not have all the facts; you do not know all of the details. If you did, you would know that the Judge of all the earth does right. We are wrong; He is right.

And the LORD said, If I find in Sodom fifty righteous within the city, then I will spare all the place for their sakes [Gen. 18:26].

And Abraham thinks this over.

And Abraham answered and said, Behold now, I have taken upon me to speak unto the Lord, which am but dust and ashes:

Peradventure there shall lack five of the fifty righteous: wilt thou destroy all the city for lack of five? And he said, If I find there forty and five, I will not destroy it [Gen. 18:27–28].

In other words, Abraham says, "If there are forty-five righteous left, would You destroy the city for forty-five?" And God tells him, "If I find there forty and five, I will not destroy it." This makes the man a little bit bolder, and he says to the Lord, "Suppose there are forty?" The very interesting thing is that God says, "I will not destroy it for forty." And Abraham keeps on bringing the number down. He says, "How about thirty?" God says, "If there are thirty there, I still won't do it." Abraham says, "Suppose there are twenty there?" God says, "I'll not destroy it." Abraham is overwhelmed now, and he takes another plunge: "Suppose there are ten righteous there. Would You destroy it if there are ten?" And God says, "If there are ten righteous in the city, I will not destroy it."

And the LORD went his way, as soon as he had left communing with Abraham: and Abraham returned unto his place [Gen. 18:33].

Now the question arises: Why didn't Abraham come on down below ten? I'll tell you why: At this point he is afraid that Lot is lost, and this disturbs him a great deal; so he is not going to come down any further. But he could have come down to one. He could have said, "Lord, if there is one in that city who is righteous, would You destroy the city?" Do you know what God would have said? He would have said, "If there is one who is righteous in that city, I am going to get him out of that city, because I would not destroy a righteous man with the city." How do I know that is the way it would have been? Because that is the way it worked out. There was one righteous man there—Abraham didn't believe it, but God knew him—and that one was Lot. God said to Lot, "Get out of the city. I cannot destroy it until you are out."

Do you know that the Great Tribulation period cannot come as long as the church is in the world? It just cannot come, my friend, because Christ bore our judgment, and the Great Tribulation is part of the judgment that is coming. This is the reason that the church cannot go through it. This is a glorious picture of that truth. We are going to see that Sodom and Gomorrah are a picture of the world—and what a picture! What a condition the world is in today—it is very much like Sodom and Gomorrah. That does not mean that the Lord is going to come tomorrow. I do not know—and no one else knows—when He will come. But He could come tomorrow, and it certainly would be in keeping with the carrying out of the picture which is before us here in Genesis.

CHAPTER 19

THEME: The angels visit Lot; destruction of the Cities of the Plain

The preceding chapter was a picture of blessed Christian fellowship with God. But now the picture changes: We leave Hebron on the plains of Mamre where Abraham dwells and we go to the city of Sodom where Lot dwells. In this chapter Lot leaves Sodom with his wife and two daughters, and Sodom and Gomorrah are destroyed. Lot's wife turns to a pillar of salt, and then we have Lot's awful sin with his two daughters.

In chapter 19 we have a picture of that which is "the blasted life." Don't forget that this man Lot happens to be a righteous man. It is hard to believe that; if I had only this record in Genesis, I wouldn't believe it. But Simon Peter, in his epistle, says of Lot, ". . . that righteous man . . . vexed his righteous soul from day to day with their unlawful deeds" (2 Pet. 2:8). Lot lived in Sodom, but he never was happy there. It was a tragic day for him when he moved to Sodom, because he lost his family—he lost all of them if you look at the total picture. It is tragic.

There is many a man today who may be a saved man, but due to his life style or where he lives, he loses his family, his influence, and his testimony. I have been a pastor for quite a few years, and I know Christians like Lot. Not too long ago, the son of a leader in a church which I served said to me that all he was doing was waiting for his dad to die in order to repudiate the Christian life. He thought the whole thing was phony; all he could see was hypocrisy. Of course, all he was doing was telling about his home. What a phony his dad must be! That man has lost his son, and he has lost his influence in other places, I can assure you. But I would not question his salvation. I think the man trusts Christ, but you would never know it by his life. Poor Lot! How tragic this is! This is one of two very sordid chapters in the Book of Genesis.

THE ANGELS VISIT LOT

And there came two angels to Sodom at even; and Lot sat in the gate of Sodom: and Lot seeing them rose up to meet them; and he bowed himself with his face toward the ground [Gen. 19:1].

These two angels visit Lot in Sodom to announce judgment. Notice that Lot was sitting in the gate of Sodom. I cannot let that go by without calling attention to the fact that the ones who sat in the gate of a city were the judges. This man Lot not only moved to Sodom, but he also got into politics down there. Here he is, a petty judge sitting in the gate.

And he said, Behold now, my lords, turn in, I pray you, into your servant's house, and tarry all night, and wash your feet, and ye shall rise up early, and go on your ways. And they said, Nay; but we will abide in the street all night [Gen. 19:2].

These two men must have had dirty feet. Of course, if you had walked from the plains of Mamre down into Sodom wearing nothing but sandals, your feet would need washing, also. Again, I call your attention to this custom of that day which was practiced by those who extended hospitality to strangers.

Lot was a hospitable man. When these strangers came, he invited them to his home, and they came in. At first, however, they were reluctant. "And they said, Nay; but we will abide in the street all night." In other words, they said, "We'll just stay outside. We don't want to inconvenience you." And they said this for a purpose, of course.

And he pressed upon them greatly; and they turned in unto him, and entered into his house; and he made them a feast, and did bake unleavened bread, and they did eat [Gen. 19:3].

Now these men have another feast. They had a feast with Abraham; they now have a feast with Lot.

They had brought out something when they said, "We'll stay on the street and just sleep in the park," and Lot says to them, "You don't do that in Sodom. It's dangerous! Your life wouldn't be worth a thing if you did that." May I say that maybe Los Angeles ought to change its name to Sodom. It would not be safe for you to sleep on the streets of Los Angeles; in fact, it is not safe at all to be on the streets of Los Angeles at night. Many women who live alone will not come out to church at night. One dear saint of God told me, "I just lock my door at dark, Brother McGee, and I do not open that door until the next morning at daylight. It's not safe in my neighborhood to even walk on the street." The days of Sodom and Gomorrah are here again, and practically for the same reason. Lot says, "No, men, do not stay on the street. It wouldn't be safe for you." When he "pressed upon them," they came in.

> **But before they lay down, the men of the city, even the men of Sodom, compassed the house round, both old and young, all the people from every quarter:**

> **And they called unto Lot, and said unto him, Where are the men which came in to thee this night? bring them out unto us, that we may know them [Gen. 19:4–5].**

This is a sickening scene which reveals the degradation of this city—the city of Sodom. The name that has been put on this sin from that day to this is *sodomy*. Apparently there was no attempt made in the city of Sodom to have a church for this crowd and to tell them that they were all right in spite of the fact that they practiced this thing. May I say to you that the Word of God is specific on this, and you cannot tone it down. Sodomy is an awful sin.

When this man Lot had gone down into the city of Sodom, he did not realize what kind of city it was—I'm sure of that. He got down there and found out that perversion was the order of the day, and he brought up his children, his sons and daughters, in that atmosphere. When he earlier had pitched his tent toward Sodom, he had looked down there and had seen the lovely streets and boulevards and parks and public buildings. And he had seen the folk as they were on the outside, but he had not seen what they really were. The sin of this city is so great that God is now going to judge it. God is going to destroy the city.

Let's draw a sharp line here. There is a new attitude toward sin today. There is a gray area where sin is not really as black as we once thought it was. The church has compromised until it is pitiful. In Southern California we have a church made up of those who are homosexuals, and, lo and behold, they all admit that the pastor of the church is one also! May I say to you, the lesson of Sodom and Gomorrah is a lesson for this generation. God is *not* accepting this kind of church.

The idea today seems to be that you can become a child of God and continue on in sin. God says that is impossible—you cannot do that, and this city of Sodom is an example of that fact. Paul asks the question: "Shall we continue in sin, that grace may abound?" And the answer is "God forbid," or, Let it not be (see Rom. 6:1–2). The idea that you can be a Christian and go on in sin is a tremendous mistake, especially to make light of it, as I judge is being done in this particular case.

This is what they were doing in Sodom and Gomorrah—and God destroyed these cities. Don't say that we have a primitive view of God in Genesis but that we have a better one today. Don't argue that, after all, Jesus received sinners. He sure did, but when He got through with them, He had changed them. The harlot who came to Him was no longer in that business. When she came to God, she changed. That is the thing that happened to other sinners. A publican came to Him, and he left the seat of customs. He gave up that which was crooked when he came to the Lord. If you have come to Christ, you will be changed. Many people write and try to explain to me that we are living in a new day and I need to wake up. My friend, we are living in a new day, but it just happens to be Sodom and Gomorrah all over again.

> And Lot went out at the door unto them, and shut the door after him,
>
> And said, I pray you, brethren, do not so wickedly [Gen. 19:6-7].

The men of Sodom were outside the door, asking that these guests in the home of Lot be turned over to them. Lot said, "I pray you, brethren, do not so wickedly." That is the way Lot looked at it, and he had been down there in Sodom a long time. It wasn't new morality to him; it was just old sin.

> Behold now, I have two daughters which have not known man; let me, I pray you, bring them out unto you, and do ye to them as is good in your eyes: only unto these men do nothing; for therefore came they under the shadow of my roof [Gen. 19:8].

When a man entertained a guest in that day, he was responsible for him. Lot was willing to make this kind of sacrifice to protect his guests!

> And they said, Stand back. And they said again, This one fellow came in to sojourn, and he will needs be a judge: now will we deal worse with thee, than with them. And they pressed sore upon the man, even Lot, and came near to break the door [Gen. 19:9].

"And they said again, This one fellow came in to sojourn, and he will needs be a judge: . . ." You see, Lot was advancing in the political arena there.

> But the men put forth their hand, and pulled Lot into the house to them, and shut to the door.
>
> And they smote the men that were at the door of the house with blindness, both small and great: so that they wearied themselves to find the door [Gen. 19:10-11].

If Lot's guests had not done this, both they and Lot would have been destroyed, because that was the intention of the men of Sodom.

And the men said unto Lot, Hast thou here any besides? son in law, and thy sons, and thy daughters, and whatsoever thou hast in the city, bring them out of this place:

For we will destroy this place, because the cry of them is waxen great before the face of the LORD; and the LORD hath sent us to destroy it.

And Lot went out, and spake unto his sons in law, which married his daughters, and said, Up, get you out of this place; for the LORD will destroy this city. But he seemed as one that mocked unto his sons in law [Gen. 19:12–14].

Lot is in a very bad situation. He had spent years down in the city of Sodom. He had learned to tolerate this sort of thing, although he calls it wickedness. He had seen his sons and daughters grow up, and they apparently had married among people with those ethical standards. When the time came that Lot got this word from the Lord to leave the city, he went to his sons-in-law and said, "Let's get out of here. God is going to destroy this city." They laughed at him. They ridiculed him. I suppose they knew that the week before Lot had invested a little money in real estate there. He had lived so long as one of them, without any real difference, that they took his warning as a big joke. This man was out of the will of God in this place, and he had no witness for God. He did not win anybody for the Lord in this city. The same principle is true today: when you go down to their level, my friend, you do not win them. I think that that is being clearly demonstrated in this hour.

Frankly, I would agree with Abraham that this man Lot wasn't saved, but remember what Peter said: "And turning the cities of Sodom and Gomorrah into ashes condemned them with an overthrow, making them an ensample unto those that after should live ungodly; And delivered just Lot, vexed with the filthy conversation of the wicked: (For that righteous man dwelling among them, in seeing and hearing, vexed his righteous soul from day to day with their unlawful deeds)" (2 Pet. 2:6–8). I tell you, Lot never enjoyed it down there in Sodom. Now that he is going to leave the city, he cannot get anyone to leave with him except his wife and two single daughters.

> **And when the morning arose, then the angels hastened Lot, saying, Arise, take thy wife, and thy two daughters, which are here; lest thou be consumed in the iniquity of the city.**
>
> **And while he lingered, the men laid hold upon his hand, and upon the hand of his wife, and upon the hand of his two daughters; the LORD being merciful unto him: and they brought him forth, and set him without the city [Gen. 19:15–16].**

Here is a man who was God's man in spite of everything. If I only had the Book of Genesis, I am not sure I would believe that Lot was saved, but since Peter calls him a righteous man, we know that he was. Lot had become righteous because he had followed Abraham—he believed God, and he had offered the sacrifices. God extends mercy unto Lot, and he now believes God and gets out of the city.

> **And it came to pass, when they had brought them forth abroad, that he said, Escape for thy life; look not behind thee, neither stay thou in all the plain; escape to the mountain, lest thou be consumed.**
>
> **And Lot said unto them, Oh, not so, my Lord:**
>
> **Behold now, thy servant hath found grace in thy sight, and thou hast magnified thy mercy, which thou hast shewed unto me in saving my life; and I cannot escape to the mountain, lest some evil take me, and I die [Gen. 19:17–19].**

Even Lot didn't want to leave. He would get out of the city, but he couldn't make it to the mountain.

> **Behold now, this city is near to flee unto, and it is a little one: Oh, let me escape thither, (is it not a little one?) and my soul shall live [Gen. 19:20].**

This city was a little place called Zoar, and that is where Lot went. You see, this man came out of Sodom, but he did not come clean even out of there. And, of course, he got into a great deal of trouble at that particular time.

DESTRUCTION OF THE CITIES OF THE PLAIN

God destroyed the cities of Sodom and Gomorrah, and we are told two things, one concerning his wife and the other concerning his daughters. Concerning his wife we read:

> **But his wife looked back from behind him, and she became a pillar of salt [Gen. 19:26].**

I think this verse has been greatly misunderstood. Why in the world did Mrs. Lot turn and look back? I think that the reason is twofold. First of all, she turned and looked back because she did not want to leave Sodom. She loved Sodom. She loved Lot, too, but it was a *lot* of Sodom that she loved. And she didn't want to leave it. She was probably a member of the country club, the sewing club, and the Shakespeare club. In fact, there wasn't a club in town that she was not a member of. She just loved these little get-togethers in the afternoon. I'm not sure but what they met and studied religion in a nice little religious club also. She was right in the thick of it all, my friend, and she didn't want to leave. Her heart was in Sodom. Her body walked out, but she surely left her heart there.

This is a tremendous lesson for us today. I hear a great many Christians talking about how they want to see the Lord come, but they are not living as if they mean it. On Sunday morning, it is difficult to get them to leave their lovely home. And on Sunday night, they are not going to leave their lovely home because they love television, too. They have a color television, and they are going to look at the pro grams on Sunday night because there are some good ones then. But when the Lord comes, my friend, you are going to leave the television; you are going to leave that lovely home; you are going to leave everything. I have just one question to ask you: Will it break your heart to leave all of this down here?

I have asked myself that question many times. To be honest with you, I am not anxious to leave. I would love to stay. I have my friends and loved ones whom I want to be with. And I have the radio ministry that I want to continue. I'll be frank with you, I hope the Lord will just let me stay here awhile longer. But I also want to be able to say that when He does call, I will not have a thing down here which will break my heart to leave—not a thing. I love my home too, but I would just as soon go off and leave it. How do you feel about that today? Mrs. Lot turned and looked back, and this is one of the explanations.

The other reason that she looked back is simply that she did not believe God. God had said, "Leave the city, and don't look back." Lot didn't look back; he believed God. But Mrs. Lot did not believe God. She was not a believer, and so she didn't really make it out of the city. She was turned to a pillar of salt.

I am not going to go into the story of Lot's two daughters in verses 31–38. It is as sordid as it can be. Frankly, Lot did not do well in moving down to the city of Sodom. He lost everything except his own soul. His life is a picture of a great many people who will not judge the sins of their lives. They are saved, "yet so as by fire." The Lord has said in a very definite way to these folk who have put all their eggs in a basket like this that if they will not judge their sin down here, He *will* judge it. Apparently, that was the case in Lot's story.

I want to conclude this chapter by looking at Abraham. What did Abraham think of all this?

And Abraham gat up early in the morning to the place where he stood before the LORD:

**And he looked toward Sodom and Gomorrah, and
toward all the land of the plain, and beheld, and, lo, the
smoke of the country went up as the smoke of a furnace
[Gen. 19:27–28].**

When Abraham looked down toward Sodom, I think his heart was
sad. I am not sure whether or not he knew that Lot had escaped. He
probably learned about it later on. When he looked down there, he
probably was sad for Lot's sake, but Abraham had not invested a dime
down there. When judgment came, it did not disturb him one whit
because he wasn't in love with the things of Sodom and the things of
the world.

Remember that we are told, "Love not the world, neither the things
that are in the world . . ." (1 John 2:15). I sometimes preach a sermon
which I have entitled "Sightseeing in Sodom." First, I look at Sodom
through the eyes of Lot himself: he sure had a wrong view of it. And
then of Mrs. Lot: she fell in love with it. You can also sightsee in
Sodom with Abraham: he lost nothing down there. Finally, you can
go through Sodom with the Lord and see it as He sees it. It is too bad
that the church today is not looking at the sin of sodomy as God looks
at it. I do not think it is any more prevalent today than it has been in
the past, but there is a tremendous percentage of our population who
are homosexuals engaging in perversion. We speak of it in a more can-
did manner than we ever have, and it is something that is right in our
midst.

What is to be the attitude of the Christian toward homosexuality?
Even Lot in his day said, "You are doing wickedly." And God judged
it. Isn't it enough for the child of God to know that he cannot compro-
mise with this type of thing? This is a *sin!* The world indulges in it
and then calls it a sickness. The same thing is said about the alco-
holic. Sure, he's sick. Of course, he's sick. But what made him take
that first drink and continue to drink until he became sick? *Sin* did it,
my friend. Sin is the problem, and homosexuality is a sin. It is so
labeled in the first chapter of Romans where God says He gave them
up (see Rom. 1:18–32). Genesis 19 is a very important chapter for this
present generation in which we are living today.

CHAPTER 20

THEME: Abraham misrepresents Sarah

Chapter 20 seems about as necessary as a fifth leg on a cow. It is a chapter that you feel as if you would like to leave out, because in it Abraham repeats the same sin which he committed when he went down into the land of Egypt and lied concerning Sarah, saying, "She is my sister." It is the same sordid story, but this chapter is put here for a very important reason. Abraham and Sarah are going to have to deal with this sin before they can have Isaac, before they can have the blessing. May I say to you, until you and I are willing to deal with the sin in our lives, there is no blessing for us.

ABRAHAM MISREPRESENTS SARAH

I am going to hit just the high points of chapter 20.

> **And Abraham journeyed from thence toward the south country, and dwelled between Kadesh and Shur, and sojourned in Gerar.**
>
> **And Abraham said of Sarah his wife, She is my sister: and Abimelech king of Gerar sent, and took Sarah [Gen. 20:1–2].**

This is quite interesting. Do you think that Sarah was beautiful? Well, at this time she is almost ninety years old, and she's beautiful. Not many senior citizens can qualify in this particular department.

Notice also that Abraham is getting quite far south in the land. He has gone beyond Kadesh-Barnea where the children of Israel later came up from Egypt and refused to enter the land. Abraham has gone down to Gerar, which I do not think he should have done, but be that as it may, he lies about Sarah again.

I want you notice Abraham's confession because this is the thing which makes this chapter important and reveals the fact that Abraham and Sarah cannot have Isaac until they deal with this sin that is in their lives—and it goes way back.

And Abraham said, Because I thought, Surely the fear of God is not in this place; and they will slay me for my wife's sake [Gen. 20:11].

Abraham is now talking to Abimelech who is greatly disturbed that Abraham would do a thing like lying about his wife. Again, Abraham was not trusting God. He felt that he was moving down into a godless place, but he finds out that Abimelech has a high sense of what is right and wrong. Abimelech puts a tremendous value upon character and apparently is a man who knows God. Poor Abraham doesn't look good by the side of Abimelech here.

And yet indeed she is my sister; she is the daughter of my father, but not the daughter of my mother; and she became my wife [Gen. 20:12].

Abraham lets it all out now. He says, "To tell the truth, it's half a lie. Sarah is my half sister, and she is my wife."

And it came to pass, when God caused me to wander from my father's house, that I said unto her, This is thy kindness which thou shalt shew unto me; at every place whither we shall come, say of me, He is my brother [Gen. 20:13].

Abraham did not have complete confidence and trust in God, and so when they started out, he and Sarah made a pact that anywhere they went where it looked as if Abraham might be killed because of his wife, Sarah would say that Abraham was her brother. Abraham and Sarah thought that that would keep Abraham from being killed. They made that little agreement, and they had used it down in Egypt, and here they have used it again. This sin must be dealt with before God is going to hear and answer Abraham's prayer in sending a son. Isaac will not be born until this is dealt with.

How many Christians are there who will not judge sin in their lives, and as a result, there is no blessing in their lives? If those who are in places of leadership in our fundamental churches would confess their sins and deal with the sins that are in their lives, I frankly believe that we could have revival. I do not believe there will be any blessing until sin is dealt with. Listen to Paul in 1 Corinthians: "But let a man examine himself, and so let him eat of that bread, and drink of that cup. For he that eateth and drinketh unworthily, eateth and drinketh damnation to himself, not discerning the Lord's body. For this cause many are weak and sickly among you, and many sleep. For if we would judge ourselves, we should not be judged. But when we are judged, we are chastened of the Lord, that we should not be condemned with the world" (1 Cor. 11:28–32). Blessing is being withheld from the church and from the lives of many believers because we will not deal with the sin in our lives. This is a tremendous spiritual lesson here in the twentieth chapter of the Book of Genesis.

CHAPTER 21

THEME: The birth of Isaac; Hagar and Ishmael cast out; Abraham and Abimelech at Beer-sheba

In the preceding chapter, we saw the sin that must be dealt with, confessed, and put away before Isaac could be born to Abraham and Sarah. Now in chapter 21 we have the birth of Isaac.

THE BIRTH OF ISAAC

And the Lord visited Sarah as he had said, and the Lord did unto Sarah as he had spoken.

For Sarah conceived, and bare Abraham a son in his old age, at the set time of which God had spoken to him [Gen. 21:1-2].

You will notice that there is a very striking similarity between the birth of Isaac and the birth of Christ. I believe that the birth of Isaac was given to us to set before mankind this great truth before Christ came. Isaac was born at the set time God had promised, and Paul says, "But when the fulness of the time was come, God sent forth his Son, made of a woman, made under the law" (Gal. 4:4).

And Abraham called the name of his son that was born unto him, whom Sarah bare to him, Isaac.

And Abraham circumcised his son Isaac being eight days old, as God had commanded him.

And Abraham was an hundred years old, when his son Isaac was born unto him.

And Sarah said, God hath made me to laugh, so that all that hear will laugh with me.

And she said, Who would have said unto Abraham, that Sarah should have given children suck? for I have born him a son in his old age [Gen. 21:3-7].

There are some very remarkable truths here that we need to lay hold of. First of all, the birth of Isaac was a miraculous birth. It was contrary to nature. In the fourth chapter of Romans, Paul writes that Abraham ". . . considered not his own body now dead . . neither yet the deadness of Sarah's womb" (Rom. 4:19). Out of death God brings forth life: this is a miraculous birth. We need to call attention to the fact that God did not flash the supernatural birth of Christ on the world as being something new. He began to prepare men for it, and therefore way back here at the birth of Isaac we have a miraculous birth.

We also find here that God had to deal with both Sarah and Abraham They had to recognize that they could do nothing, that it would be impossible for them to have a child. Abraham is 100 years old; Sarah is 90 years old. In other words, the birth of Isaac must be a birth that they really have nothing to do with.

And the child grew, and was weaned: and Abraham made a great feast the same day that Isaac was weaned [Gen. 21:8].

This little fellow first lived by feeding on his mother's milk, but there came a day when he had to be weaned. Even this has a lesson for us. When mamma is getting the bottle ready for the little baby in the crib, everything in his entire body is working. He's got his feet up in the air, he's got his hands up in the air, and he's yelling at the top of his voice—he wants his bottle! "As newborn babes, desire the sincere milk of the word, that ye may grow thereby" (1 Peter 2:2). It is wonderful to be a new Christian with an appetite like that for the milk of the Word. But the day comes when you are ready to start growing up as a believer. Instead of just reading Psalm 23 and John 14—wonderful as they are—try reading through the entire Bible. Grow up. Don't be a babe all of the time. Notice God's admonishment in Hebrews 5:13-14

"For every one that useth milk is unskilful in the word of righteousness: for he is a babe. But strong meat belongeth to them that are of full age . . ." Grow up, friend.

HAGAR AND ISHMAEL CAST OUT

And Sarah saw the son of Hagar the Egyptian, which she had born unto Abraham, mocking.

Wherefore she said unto Abraham, Cast out this bondwoman and her son: for the son of this bondwoman shall not be heir with my son, even with Isaac [Gen. 21:9–10].

The coming of this little boy Isaac into the home sure did produce a great deal of difficulty. We find that the boy who was the son of Hagar, Ishmael, was mocking. We begin now to see the nature and the character of Ishmael. Up to this point, he seems to be a pretty nice boy, but now, with the appearance of this other son in the family, Ishmael really shows his true colors.

This is an illustration, by the way, of the fact that a believer has two natures. Until you are converted, you have an old nature, and that old nature controls you. You do what you want to do. As the old secular song put it, you are "doing what comes naturally." What you do that comes naturally is not always the nicest sort of thing. But when you are born again, you receive a new nature. And when you receive a new nature, that is where the trouble always begins. Paul writes in the seventh chapter of Romans of the battle going on between the old nature and the new nature: "For the good that I would I do not: but the evil which I would not, that I do" (Rom. 7:19). That is, the new nature doesn't want to, but the old nature wants to do it, and the old nature is in control. The time comes when you have to make a decision as to which nature you are going to live by. You must make a determination in this matter of yielding to the Lord. You either have to permit the Holy Spirit to move in your life, or else you have to go through life controlled by the flesh. There is no third alternative for the child of

God. The son of the bondwoman must be put out. That is exactly what we have here in Genesis: the son of the bondwoman Hagar had to be put out.

And the thing was very grievous in Abraham's sight be-cause of his son [Gen. 21:11].

After all, as far as the flesh is concerned, Ishmael is Abraham's son just as much as Isaac is. Isaac has just been born, and a little bitty baby doesn't know too much about him yet. But this boy Ishmael has been in the home for a good many years—he's a teen-ager now, and Abraham is attached to him. The thing is very grievous if Abraham is going to have to send him away. Again, I go back to that which we said before: God did not approve of the thing which Sarah and Abraham did, and God cannot accept Ishmael. This is sin. God just did not approve of it, and He doesn't intend to approve of it at all. It was a heartbreak to Abraham, but in order to relieve the embarrassment, he had to send that boy away. Poor Sarah just couldn't take it with this older boy around mocking her.

As a believer you cannot live in harmony with both natures. You are going to have to make a decision. James says, "A double-minded man is unstable in all his ways" (James 1:8). This explains the instability and the insecurity among many Christians today. They want to go with the world, and yet they want to go with the Lord. They are spiritual schizophrenics, trying to do both—and you cannot do that. The Greeks had a race in which they put two horses together, and the rider would put one foot on one horse and the other foot on the other horse, and the race would start. Well, it was a great race as long as the horses were together. You and I have two natures—one is a black horse, and the other is a white horse. It would be great if they would go together, but they just will not work together. The white horse goes one way and the black horse another way. When they do this, you and I have to make up our minds which one we are going with—whether we are going to live by the old nature or the new nature. This is why we are told to yield ourselves: "yield yourselves unto God . . . and your members as instruments of righteousness unto God" (Rom

6:13). Paul goes on to say that what the law could not do through the weakness of the flesh, the Spirit of God can now accomplish (see Rom. 8:3–4). The law tried to control man's old nature and failed. Now the Spirit of God, empowering the new nature, can accomplish what the law could never do.

The character of Ishmael, the son of Hagar, begins to be revealed. This is the nature that we find manifested later on in that nation, a nation that is antagonistic and whose hand is against his brother. This has been the picture of him down through the centuries.

In the birth of Isaac, as I have already suggested, we have a foreshadowing of the birth of the Lord Jesus Christ. God did not suddenly spring the virgin birth on mankind. He had prepared us by several miraculous births before this, including the birth of John the Baptist, the birth even of Samson, and here the birth of Isaac. I would like to call your attention to the remarkable comparison between the births of Isaac and of the Lord Jesus Christ.

(1) The birth of Isaac and the birth of Christ had both been promised. When God called Abraham out of Ur of the Chaldees twenty-five years earlier, God had said to him, "I am going to give a son to you and Sarah." Now twenty-five years have gone by, and God has made good His promise. God also said to the nation Israel, "A virgin shall conceive and bring forth a son." When the day came that Jesus was born in Bethlehem, it was a fulfillment of prophecy. Both births had been promised.

(2) With both births there was a long interval between the promise and the fulfillment. Actually, there were about twenty-five years from the time God promised it until the birth of Isaac. With the birth of Christ, you could go back many generations. For example, God had promised that there would come One in David's line—and that was a thousand years before Christ was born. This is quite a remarkable parallel here.

(3) The announcements of the births seemed incredulous and impossible to Sarah and to Mary. You will recall that the servants of the Lord visited Abraham as they were on the way to Sodom, and they announced the birth of Isaac. It just seemed impossible. Sarah laughed and said, "This thing just can't be. It is beyond belief." And,

after all, who was the first one to raise a question about the virgin birth? It was Mary herself. When the angel made the announcement, she said, ". . . How shall this be, seeing I know not a man?" (Luke 1:34).

(4) Both Isaac and Jesus were named before their births. Abraham and Sarah were told that they were going to have a son and that they were going to name him Isaac. And with the birth of the Lord Jesus, we find that He was also named beforehand. The angel said to Joseph, ". . . thou shalt call his name JESUS: for he shall save his people from their sins" (Matt. 1:21).

(5) Both births occurred at God's appointed time. Verse 2 of this chapter says that at the set time which God had spoken to them of, Sarah brought forth Isaac. And regarding the birth of Jesus, we note that Paul says, "But when the fulness of the time was come, God sent forth his Son, made of a woman, made under the law" (Gal. 4:4).

(6) Both births were miraculous. The birth of Isaac was a miraculous birth, and, certainly, the birth of the Lord Jesus was—no man had any part in that.

(7) Both sons were a particular joy of their fathers. We read that "Abraham called the name of his son that was born unto him, whom Sarah bare to him, Isaac," meaning laughter. This was the name he gave his son because back at the time when God made the announcement, he laughed because of his sheer joy in it all. Referring to the Lord Jesus, we read that the Father spoke out of heaven and said, ". . . This is my beloved Son, in whom I am well pleased" (Matt. 3:17) Both sons were a joy.

(8) Both sons were obedient to their fathers, even unto death. In chapter 22 we are going to see that this boy Isaac was offered up by his father. He was not a small boy of eight or nine years. Isaac just happened to be about thirty-three years old when this took place, and he was obedient to his father even unto death. That was true of Isaac, and that was certainly true of the Lord Jesus Christ. There is a marvelous picture of the birth and life of Christ in the birth and life of Isaac.

(9) Finally, the miraculous birth of Isaac is a picture of the resurrection of Christ. We have already noted Paul's words that Abraham "considered not his own body now *dead* . . . neither yet the *deadness*

of Sarah's womb" (Rom. 4:19). Out of death came life—that's resurrection, you see. After Paul emphasizes this, he goes on to say of the Lord Jesus, "Who was delivered for our offences, and was raised again for our justification" (Rom. 4:25). We have in Isaac quite a remarkable picture of the Lord Jesus Christ.

Now we find how God graciously deals with Abraham and also with Hagar and her son Ishmael.

> **And God said unto Abraham, Let it not be grievous in thy sight because of the lad, and because of thy bondwoman; in all that Sarah hath said unto thee, hearken unto her voice; for in Isaac shall thy seed be called [Gen. 21:12].**

God makes it clear to Abraham that He is not going to accept Ishmael as the son He had promised.

> **And also of the son of the bondwoman will I make a nation, because he is thy seed [Gen. 21:13].**

God had said, "Of thy seed, I will make nations to come from you," and therefore He now says that a great nation will come from this boy Ishmael also.

> **And Abraham rose up early in the morning, and took bread, and a bottle of water, and gave it unto Hagar, putting it on her shoulder, and the child, and sent her away: and she departed, and wandered in the wilderness of Beer-sheba.**

> **And the water was spent in the bottle, and she cast the child under one of the shrubs.**

> **And she went, and sat her down over against him a good way off, as it were a bowshot: for she said, Let me not see the death of the child. And she sat over against him, and lift up her voice, and wept.**

And God heard the voice of the lad; and the angel of God called to Hagar out of heaven, and said unto her, What aileth thee, Hagar? fear not; for God hath heard the voice of the lad where he is.

Arise, lift up the lad, and hold him in thine hand; for I will make him a great nation.

And God opened her eyes, and she saw a well of water; and she went, and filled the bottle with water, and gave the lad drink.

And God was with the lad; and he grew, and dwelt in the wilderness, and became an archer.

And he dwelt in the wilderness of Paran: and his mother took him a wife out of the land of Egypt [Gen. 21:14–21].

The Scriptures are going to drop the line of Ishmael and follow it no longer, but his descendants, the Arabs, are out there in the desert even today.

ABRAHAM AND ABIMELECH AT BEER-SHEBA

And it came to pass at that time, that Abimelech and Phichol the chief captain of his host spake unto Abraham, saying, God is with thee in all that thou doest:

Now therefore swear unto me here by God that thou wilt not deal falsely with me, nor with my son, nor with my son's son: but according to the kindness that I have done unto thee, thou shalt do unto me, and to the land wherein thou hast sojourned [Gen. 21:22–23].

In other words, Abimelech wants to make a contract or a treaty with this man Abraham—and they become good friends because of this.

Thus they made a covenant at Beer-sheba: then Abimelech rose up, and Phichol the chief captain of his host,
and they returned into the land of the Philistines.

And Abraham planted a grove in Beer-sheba, and
called there on the name of the LORD, the everlasting
God [Gen. 21:32–33].

Abraham is calling upon God's name everywhere he goes.

And Abraham sojourned in the Philistines' land many
days [Gen. 21:34].

We are told later that Abraham was always a stranger and a pilgrim in
this land that God had promised to him, and this is an evidence of it.

CHAPTER 22

THEME: God commands Abraham to offer Isaac; God restrains Abraham; God reaffirms His promises; Abraham returns to Beer-sheba

In this chapter we come to another great high point of the Bible. We are walking on mountain peaks in the Book of Genesis. Chapter 22 is the account of Abraham's offering of his own son. God commanded him to offer Isaac on the altar and then restrained him at the last minute when He saw that Abraham was willing to go through with it. This chapter brings us to the seventh and last appearance of God to Abraham. After this, there is nothing more that God could ask Abraham to do. This is the supreme test that He brought to this man.

If you were to designate the ten greatest chapters of the Bible, you would almost have to include Genesis 22. One of the reasons for that is that this is the first time human sacrifice is even suggested. It is in the plan and purpose of God to make it clear to man that human sacrifice is wrong. This incident reveals that. It also reveals that God requires a life to be given up in order that He might save sinners. There is no one among the children of men worthy to take that place. God's Son was the only One. It is interesting that Paul said, "God spared not His own Son," but you might add that He *did* spare the son of Abraham and did not let him go through with the sacrifice of Isaac.

This chapter compares with Psalm 22 and Isaiah 53. The first time that I saw in this chapter these great truths which depict the cross of Christ, it was breathtaking. Not only in the birth of Isaac, but now also in the sacrifice of Isaac, there is a strange similarity to the life of our Lord.

The very interesting thing is that James makes a statement concerning this incident which may seem contradictory to other parts of the Bible: "Was not Abraham our father justified by works, when he had offered Isaac his son upon the altar?" (James 2:21). For Paul makes this statement in Romans 4: "What shall we say then that Abraham our father, as pertaining to the flesh, hath found? For if Abraham were justified by works, he hath whereof to glory; but not before God. For what saith the scripture? Abraham believed God, and it was counted unto him for righteousness" (Rom. 4:1-3). Who is right? James or Paul? My answer is that both of them are right. First of all, we need to note that both of them are talking about the same thing—faith. James is talking about the works of *faith*, not the works of law. Paul is talking about justification before God, quoting the fifteenth chapter of Genesis, way back when Abraham was just getting under way in a walk of faith. At that time only God knew his heart, and God saw that Abraham believed Him: "And he (Abraham) believed in the LORD; and he counted it to him for righteousness" (Gen. 15:6). We can see that Abraham failed many times, and I am of the opinion that his neighbors might have said, "We don't see that he is righteous." But when the day came that he took his son to be offered on the altar, even the hardhearted Philistine had to admit that Abraham demonstrated his faith by his actions. James says that Abraham was justified by works. When was he justified? When he offered Isaac. But the question is going to arise: Did Abraham really offer Isaac upon the altar? Of course, the answer is that he didn't—but he was willing to. That very act of being willing is the act that James is talking about which reveals that Abraham had the works of faith. James is emphasizing the works of faith seen in this twenty-second chapter of Genesis, and Paul is talking about faith in his heart which Abraham had way back in the fifteenth chapter.

GOD COMMANDS ABRAHAM TO OFFER ISAAC

And it came to pass after these things, that God did tempt Abraham, and said unto him, Abraham: and he said, Behold, here I am [Gen. 22:1].

The word *tempt* is a little bit too strong; actually, the word means "test." James makes it very clear in his epistle that God never tempts anyone with evil. God tempts folks in the sense that He tests their faith. God did test Abraham, and He asked him to do something very strange.

And he said, Take now thy son, thine only son Isaac, whom thou lovest, and get thee into the land of Moriah; and offer him there for a burnt offering upon one of the mountains which I will tell thee of [Gen. 22:2].

Right after this chapter, we are told that Sarah was 127 years old when she died (see Gen. 23:1). When you put that down with this chapter, you find that this boy Isaac was not just a little lad. Sarah was 90 years old when Isaac was born and 127 when she died. That means that 37 years elapsed here. Since he is called a "lad" in this chapter, you would not gather that he actually was in his thirties—probably around 30 or 33 years of age.

"Take now thy son [notice how this plays upon the heartstrings of Abraham and of God Himself], thine *only* son Isaac, whom thou *lovest*." "Take now thy son"—the Lord Jesus has taken the position of the Son in the Trinity. "Thy son, thine only son"—the Lord Jesus is said to be the only begotten Son. "Thine only son Isaac, whom thou lovest"— the Lord Jesus said, "The Father loves Me."

"And get thee into the land of Moriah." It is the belief of a great many that Moriah—that is, this particular part—is the place where the temple was built centuries later and also the place that the Lord Jesus was sacrificed—right outside the city walls. When I was in Jerusalem, I had the feeling that Golgotha and the temple area were not very far apart. They belong to the same ridge. A street has been cut through there, and the ridge has been breached, but it is the same ridge, and it is called Moriah. Let's not say that the Lord Jesus died in the exact spot—we don't know—but certainly He died on the same ridge, the same mountain, on which Abraham offered Isaac.

"And offer him there for a burnt offering upon one of the mountains which I will tell thee of." The burnt offering was the offering up until the time of Mosaic law; then a sin offering and a trespass offering were given. Here the burnt offering speaks of the person of Christ, who He is. This is an offer of a human sacrifice, and, frankly, it raises this moral question: Isn't human sacrifice wrong? Yes, it is morally wrong. Had you met Abraham on that day when he was on his way with Isaac, you might have asked him, "Where are you going, Abraham?" He would have replied, "To offer Isaac as a sacrifice." And you would have then asked, "Don't you know that that is wrong?" Abraham would have said, "Yes, I've been taught that it was wrong. I know that the heathen nations around here offer human sacrifice—the Philistines offer to Molech—but I have been taught otherwise." You would then question him further, "Then why are you doing it?" and he would explain, "All I know is that God has commanded it. I don't understand it. But I've been walking with Him now for over fifty years. He has never failed me, nor has He asked me to do anything that did not prove to be the best thing. I don't understand this, but I believe that if I go all the way with Him that God will raise Isaac from the dead. I believe that He will do that."

This is a tremendous picture as Abraham takes Isaac with him:

And Abraham rose up early in the morning, and saddled his ass, and took two of his young men with him, and Isaac his son, and clave the wood for the burnt offering, and rose up, and went unto the place of which God had told him [Gen. 22:3].

Abraham takes Isaac with him, and he takes the wood for the burnt offering.

Then on the third day Abraham lifted up his eyes, and saw the place afar off [Gen. 22:4].

It took Abraham three days to get there, but remember that it was on the third day that Abraham received Isaac alive, back from the dead, as it were. That is the way that Abraham looked at it: Isaac was raised up to him the third day. What a picture we have here.

And Abraham said unto his young men, Abide ye here with the ass; and I and the lad will go yonder and worship, and come again to you [Gen. 22:5].

The transaction that is going to take place is between the father and the son, between Abraham and Isaac. And actually, God shut man out at the cross. At the time of the darkness at high noon, man was shut out. The night had come when no man could work, and during those last three hours, that cross became an altar on which the Lamb of God who taketh away the sin of the world was offered. The transaction was between the Father and the Son on that cross. Man was outside and was not participating at all. The picture is the same here: it is Abraham and Isaac alone.

> **And Abraham took the wood of the burnt offering, and laid it upon Isaac his son; and he took the fire in his hand, and a knife; and they went both of them together [Gen. 22:6].**

"Abraham took the wood . . . and laid it upon Isaac his son." Remember that Christ carried His own cross. The fire here speaks of judgment, and the knife speaks of the execution of judgment and of sacrifice.

> **And Isaac spake unto Abraham his father, and said, My father: and he said, Here I am, my son. And he said, Behold the fire and the wood: but where is the lamb for a burnt offering?**
>
> **And Abraham said, My son, God will provide himself a lamb for a burnt offering: so they went both of them together [Gen. 22:7–8].**

Verse 13 tells us that shortly after this there was a ram that was caught in the thicket by his horns, and Abraham got that ram and offered it. Abraham says here that God will provide Himself a *lamb*. But there was no *lamb* there; it was a *ram*, and there is a distinction. The Lamb was not provided until centuries later when John the Baptist marked Him out and identified Him, saying, ". . . Behold the Lamb of God, which taketh away the sin of the world" (John 1:29). "God will provide himself a lamb for a burnt offering"—it is very important to see that Abraham was speaking prophetically.

Abraham is now ready to offer this boy on the altar although he does not quite understand.

And they came to the place which God had told him of; and Abraham built an altar there, and laid the wood in order, and bound Isaac his son, and laid him on the altar upon the wood [Gen. 22:9].

Isaac is not just a little boy whom Abraham had to tie up. He is a grown man, and I believe that Isaac could have overcome Abraham if it had come to a physical encounter. But Isaac is doing this in obedience. The Lord Jesus went to the cross having said, "Not My will, but Thine be done." He went to the cross to fulfill the will of God. What a picture we have here!

And Abraham stretched forth his hand, and took the knife to slay his son [Gen. 22:10].

At this point you and I might have said, "Abraham, are you going through with it? It looks now like God is going to permit you to." He would have said, "I sure am. I've been taught that it is wrong, and I don't understand, but I've also learned to obey God."

This is a real crisis in Abraham's life. God has brought this man through four very definite crises, each of which was a real exercise of his soul, a real strain upon his heart. First of all, he was called to leave all of his relatives in Ur of the Chaldees. He was just to leave the whole group. That was a real test for Abraham. He didn't do it very well at the beginning, but, nevertheless, the break finally came. Then there was the test that came with Lot, his nephew. Abraham loved Lot—he wouldn't have been carrying Lot around with him if he hadn't. But the time came when they had to separate, and Lot went down to Sodom. Then there was the test with this boy of his, the son of Hagar, Ishmael. Abraham just cried out to God, "Oh, that Ishmael might live before Thee!" He loved that boy; he hated to be separated from him.

Now Abraham comes to this supreme test, the fourth great crisis in his life: he is asked to give up Isaac. Abraham does not quite understand all the details for the very simple reason that God has told him, "In Isaac your seed shall be called." Abraham believed God would raise Isaac from the dead (see Heb. 11:19), but as far as Abraham is concerned, he is willing to go through with the sacrifice.

GOD RESTRAINS ABRAHAM

James wrote that Abraham was justified by works when he offered up his son. But wait just a minute. Did Abraham offer his son? Does your Bible say that Abraham plunged the knife into his son? No, and mine doesn't read that way either.

> **And the angel of the Lord called unto him out of heaven, and said, Abraham, Abraham: and he said, Here am I.**

> **And he said, Lay not thine hand upon the lad, neither do thou any thing unto him: for now I know that thou fearest God, seeing thou hast not withheld thy son, thine only son from me [Gen. 22:11–12].**

Now God knows that Abraham fears Him. How does He know? By his actions, by his works; previously it was by his faith. God sees your heart—He knows whether you are genuine or not—but your neighbors and your friends do not know. They can only know by your works. That is the reason James could say that "faith without works is dead." Faith has to produce something.

God tested Abraham. I believe that any person whom God calls, any person whom God saves, any person whom God uses is going to be tested. God tested Abraham, and God tests those who are His own today. He tests you and me, and the tests are given to us to strengthen our faith, to establish us, and to make us serviceable for Him. This man Abraham is now given the supreme test, and God will not have to ask anything of him after this.

And Abraham lifted up his eyes, and looked, and behold behind him a ram caught in a thicket by his horns: and Abraham went and took the ram, and offered him up for a burnt offering in the stead of his son [Gen. 22:13].

All the way from the Garden of Eden down to the cross of Christ, the substitution was this little animal that pointed to His coming—and God would not permit human sacrifice. But when His Son came into the world, His Son went to the cross and died: "He that spared not his own Son, but delivered him up for us all, how shall he not with him also freely give us all things?" (Rom. 8:32). That cross became an altar on which the Lamb of God that taketh away the sin of the world was offered. It is very important to see that.

And Abraham called the name of that place Jehovah-jireh: as it is said to this day, In the mount of the LORD it shall be seen [Gen. 22:14].

Abraham now names this place which a great many people believe is where Solomon's temple was built. Golgotha, the place of a skull, is right there on that same ridge where the temple stood. There Abraham offered his son, and it was there that the Lord Jesus Christ was crucified. This is a glorious, wonderful thing to see. Abraham calls the name of this place Jehovah-jireh, meaning Jehovah will provide. Here is where God intervened in his behalf.

GOD REAFFIRMS HIS PROMISES

And the angel of the LORD called unto Abraham out of heaven the second time,

And said, By myself have I sworn, saith the LORD, for because thou hast done this thing, and hast not withheld thy son, thine only son [Gen. 22:15–16].

I have a question to ask: *Did* Abraham do it? No, he did not offer his son, but God says to him, "Because you have done this thing. . . ." You see, Abraham believed God, and he went far enough to let you and me know—God already knew—and to let the created universe know that he was willing to give his son. And so God counted it to him that he had done it. Abraham is justified by faith, but he is also justified before men by his works. He *demonstrated* that he had that faith.

"And hast not withheld thy son, *thine only son*." Notice how God plays upon that—because He gave His only Son.

Through this incident, God is making it clear that there will have to be a Man to stand in the gap, there will have to be a Man capable of becoming the Savior of the race if anyone is to be saved. That is a great lesson given to us in this chapter. Abraham said that God would provide Himself a Lamb, and they found a ram and offered it. But God did provide a Lamb nineteen hundred years later in Christ. God stayed Abraham's hand and did not let him go through with the sacrifice of Isaac because it would have been wrong. God spared Abraham's son, but God did not spare His own Son but gave Him up freely for us all.

That in blessing I will bless thee, and in multiplying I will multiply thy seed as the stars of the heaven, and as the sand which is upon the sea shore; and thy seed shall possess the gate of his enemies;

And in thy seed shall all the nations of the earth be blessed; because thou hast obeyed my voice [Gen. 22:17-18].

"And in *thy* seed shall all the nations of the earth be blessed." What "seed" is God talking about here? If you go to Galatians 3:16, you will find that Paul interprets what the "seed" means: "Now to Abraham and his seed were the promises made. He saith not, And to seeds, as of many; but as of one, And to thy seed, which is Christ." Thus we have the Bible's own interpretation of the "seed."

Going back to the eighth verse, we find that Paul says this: "And the scripture, foreseeing that God would justify the heathen through faith, preached before the gospel unto Abraham, saying, In thee shall all nations be blessed" (Gal. 3:8). When did God preach the gospel to Abraham? God preached the gospel to him when He called upon him to offer his son Isaac upon the altar. God says here, "In thy seed shall all the nations of the earth be blessed" and that seed is Christ. This is the gospel as it was given to Abraham if you please.

I would like to make a comment here concerning something that is customarily overlooked. We assume that Abraham, Isaac, Jacob, and all the Old Testament worthies were great men but that they were not as smart as we are, that they did not know as much as we know. However, I am of the opinion that Abraham knew a great deal more about the coming of Christ and the gospel than you and I give him credit for. In fact, the Lord Jesus said, "Your father Abraham rejoiced to see my day: and he saw it, and was glad" (John 8:56). So he must have known a great deal more than we realize. God had revealed much to Abraham, but the Savior was not yet come. We know today that He would not come for nineteen hundred years, but there on the top of Mount Moriah where Abraham offered Isaac was a picture of the offering and even of the resurrection of Christ! After God called Abraham to offer Isaac, it was three days before he even got to Moriah. God gave Isaac back to Abraham alive on the third day; so that this is a picture of both the death and resurrection of Christ. Paul says that God preached the gospel to Abraham, and certainly it was done here.

"And in thy seed shall *all* the nations of the earth be blessed." Today the gospel of Christ has gone out pretty much to all the world. There are many who have not heard—that is true even in our own midst—but nevertheless, the blessing has come to all nations. And the only blessing the nations have is through Christ.

"Because thou hast obeyed my voice." That obedience rested upon Abraham's faith, and faith always will lead to action. "Faith without works is dead."

ABRAHAM RETURNS TO BEER-SHEBA

So Abraham returned unto his young men, and they rose up and went together to Beer-sheba; and Abraham dwelt at Beer-sheba.

And it came to pass after these things, that it was told Abraham, saying, Behold, Milcah, she hath also born children unto thy brother Nahor [Gen. 22:19–20].

The remainder of this chapter gives us a little sidelight on the family of Abraham. Abraham had left his brother Nahor way back yonder in the land of Haran. His line will not be followed in the Scriptures, but it will cross the line of Abraham a little later on. We will go into that when we come to it. If you read the rest of this chapter, you will have quite an exercise in the pronunciation of names.

CHAPTER 23

In chapter 23 we see the death of Sarah and Abraham's purchase of a cave in which to bury her, the cave of Machpelah.

And Sarah was an hundred and seven and twenty years old: these were the years of the life of Sarah.

And Sarah died in Kirjath-arba; the same is Hebron in the land of Canaan: and Abraham came to mourn for Sarah, and to weep for her [Gen. 23:1–2].

Notice that Sarah's age is given as 127 years old. She was 90 when Isaac was born, which means that at the time of her death (which took place after the offering of Isaac by several years, I suppose), Isaac was 37 years old.

We are told that Sarah died in Kirjath-arba, which is Hebron. Abraham even had to buy a cave in which to bury his dead in the very land that God had given to him. Why didn't he take Sarah somewhere else to bury her? It is because the hope they have of the future is in that land. As we move on down in this chapter, we will see that although there are the arrangements for a funeral, which is not very exciting or interesting and is perhaps even a little morbid to some, it is very important to see a great truth here.

And Abraham stood up from before his dead, and spake unto the sons of Heth, saying,

I am a stranger and a sojourner with you: give me a possession of a buryingplace with you, that I may bury my dead out of my sight [Gen. 23:3–4].

Abraham calls himself a stranger and a sojourner even in the Promised Land which God had promised to give to him.

> And the children of Heth answered Abraham, saying unto him,
>
> Hear us, my lord: thou art a mighty prince among us: in the choice of our sepulchres bury thy dead; none of us shall withhold from thee his sepulchre, but that thou mayest bury thy dead [Gen. 23:5–6].

This is a very generous offer made by the children of Heth who live in this land. They probably said to Abraham, "Just pick your burying spot in any of our sepulchers—that's it. We'd be delighted to have you." Abraham had made a tremendous impression. They call him "a mighty prince." This man's influence counted for something.

> And Abraham stood up, and bowed himself to the people of the land, even to the children of Heth.
>
> And he communed with them, saying, if it be your mind that I should bury my dead out of my sight; hear me, and entreat for me to Ephron the son of Zohar,
>
> That he may give me the cave of Machpelah, which he hath, which is in the end of his field; for as much money as it is worth he shall give it me for a possession of a buryingplace amongst you [Gen. 23:7–9].

The cave of Machpelah was the place Abraham chose, but he wanted to buy it; he wanted nothing given to him. In other words, until God gives him that land, he will buy what he needs and wants. So now he actually buys a burying place.

Again I ask the question: Why didn't Abraham take Sarah somewhere else to bury her? He buried her here because it is the Promised Land, and the hope of the future is here. As you go through the Bible, you will find that there are two great hopes and two great purposes which God has. He has an *earthly* purpose, and He has a *heavenly* purpose. He has an earthly purpose; that is, this earth on which you and I live is going into eternity. It is going to be traded in on a new model. There will be a new heaven and a new earth. But there *will* be an earth, and it will be inhabited throughout eternity. This is the promise that God gave to Abraham and to those after him. God is not going to put this earth on which you and I live in the garbage can after He gets through with the program which He is carrying out today; nor is it going to be disposed of in a wrecking yard for old and battered cars. God is not going to get rid of it. He intends to trade it in on a new model. The new earth will go into eternity, and there will be people to inhabit it. This was the hope of Abraham. Abraham wanted to be buried in that land so that, when the resurrection came, he and Sarah would be raised in that land. He never knew how many were coming after him, but there are going to be literally millions raised from the dead. This is their hope. It is an earthly hope, and it will be realized.

In the Upper Room, our Lord said this to His disciples who were schooled in the Old Testament and who had the Old Testament hope: "Let not your heart be troubled: ye believe in God, believe also in me. In my Father's house are many mansions: if it were not so, I would have told you. I go to prepare a place for you. And if I go and prepare a place for you, I will come again, and receive you unto myself; that where I am, there ye may be also" (John 14:1–3). He is speaking of the New Jerusalem which He is preparing today and which is the place to which the church will go. The New Jerusalem will be the eternal abode of the church. This teaching was brand-new to the disciples, and I am afraid that it is brand-new to a great many Christians. God never told Abraham that He would take him away from this earth to heaven. Rather, He kept telling him, "I am going to give you this land." Abraham believed God, and that was the reason that he wanted Sarah buried in that land. It became the place for him to bury his dead. He intended to be buried there, and he *is* buried there.

The exact location of Abraham's burying place is at Hebron, about twenty miles south of Jerusalem. When we made a trip there, we visited the Moslem mosque which is built over that spot. Frankly, on our entire trip through that land, I never felt uncomfortable or even a little afraid, except at Hebron. We had been warned to be very careful in

Hebron, that there was a great deal of antagonism toward tourists and, actually, toward everyone who did not belong there. Of course, they allowed us to visit the mosque because it meant tourist dollars. After we went in, we looked through a little hole in the floor and down into the cave where Abraham and Sarah, Isaac and Rebekah, Jacob and Leah are all supposed to be buried. (Rachel is buried at Bethlehem.) These folk are all buried in Israel because of their hope of being raised from the dead in that land. It is an earthly hope. Our hope as New Testament believers is a heavenly hope. I trust that that is clear to you so that you can understand why this burial was so important to Abraham at this particular time.

Abraham now makes a deal to buy the cave. Notice the transaction:

And Ephron dwelt among the children of Heth: and Ephron the Hittite answered Abraham in the audience of the children of Heth, even of all that went in at the gate of his city, saying,

Nay, my lord, hear me: the field give I thee, and the cave that is therein, I give it thee; in the presence of the sons of my people give I it thee: bury thy dead.

And Abraham bowed down himself before the people of the land [Gen. 23:10–12].

Notice Abraham and the generosity of these people and of this man Ephron in particular. They certainly were polite in that day. We have the impression that these were cavemen who carried clubs around ready to club each other. If Abraham, Isaac, Jacob, and the other Old Testament saints—even the men who are mentioned in this chapter— were in Los Angeles today and could go back and report to their folk, I think they would say, "Do you know that our offspring are a bunch of cavemen? They're highly uncivilized! They are rude and crude and a disgrace." I think they would say that of us, but *we* have the advantage that we can talk about them. It is interesting to note how polite they are. "And Abraham bowed down himself before the people of the land."

And he spake unto Ephron in the audience of the people
of the land, saying, But if thou wilt give it, I pray thee,
hear me: I will give thee money for the field; take it of
me, and I will bury my dead there.

And Ephron answered Abraham, saying unto him,

My lord, hearken unto me: the land is worth four hundred shekels of silver; what is that betwixt me and thee?
bury therefore thy dead.

And Abraham hearkened unto Ephron; and Abraham
weighed to Ephron the silver, which he had named in
the audience of the sons of Heth, four hundred shekels of
silver, current money with the merchant [Gen. 23:13–
16].

That is, Abraham paid for the field and cave in the legal tender of that
day.

And the field of Ephron, which was in Machpelah,
which was before Mamre, the field, and the cave which
was therein, and all the trees that were in the field, that
were in all the borders round about, were made sure

Unto Abraham for a possession in the presence of the
children of Heth, before all that went in at the gate of his
city.

And after this, Abraham buried Sarah his wife in the
cave of the field of Machpelah before Mamre: the same
is Hebron in the land of Canaan.

And the field, and the cave that is therein, were made
sure unto Abraham for a possession of a buryingplace
by the sons of Heth [Gen. 23:17–20].

Apparently, this place is where the mosque is built at Hebron today. It
is considered either the second or third most important mosque in the

world of Islam. They have many mosques in Cairo and other places, and the ones I have seen are absolutely beautiful. The most important one, of course, would be at Mecca. I am not sure whether the one at Hebron or the one at Jerusalem would be number two, but the other would then be number three. You can see how important this is, because the Arabs all trace their lineage back to Abraham.

CHAPTER 24

THEME: A bride for Isaac

We have come in chapter 24 to a major break in this second division of Genesis. The first division (chapters 1—11) deals with *four great events*. The second and final division (chapters 12—50), deals with *four outstanding individuals*. Specifically, in Genesis 12—23 we have Abraham, the man of faith. Now in chapters 24—26 we have Isaac, the beloved son. There are three great events in the life of Isaac, and we have already seen two of them. The first was his birth, and the second was his being offered by Abraham. The third is the obtaining of his bride. They say there are three great events in a man's life—his birth, his marriage, and his death—and that he has no choice except with the second one, marriage. Sometimes a man doesn't seem to have much choice in that connection either, but, nevertheless, these are the three great events in a man's life.

We come now to the story of how Isaac secured his bride. Abraham sends his trusted servant back to the land of Haran in Mesopotamia to get a bride for Isaac—and we will see the success of the servant in securing Rebekah. This is a very wonderful love story. It reveals that God is interested in the man whom you marry, young lady, and He is interested in the young lady whom you marry, young man.

There are two institutions that God has given to the human family: one is marriage, and the other is human government (God permits man to rule himself today). These are two universal and very important institutions. When these are broken, a society will fall apart. The home is the backbone of any society—God knew that—and He established marriage, intending that it give strength and stability to society. The same thing is true relative to human government—a government must have the power to take human life in order to protect human life—that is the purpose of it. Because human life is sacred, God gave such laws.

The point here is that God is interested in your love story, and it is wonderful when you bring God into it. The first miracle that our Lord performed was at a wedding in Cana of Galilee. I do not know how many weddings He went to, but He went to that one.

The twenty-fourth chapter of Genesis is one of the richest sections of the Word of God because it tells a love story that goes way back to the very beginning. A very dramatic account is given here of the way that a bride was secured for Isaac, and again, a fantastic spiritual picture is also presented to us. There are two things that I want you to notice as we go through this chapter. One is the leading of the Lord in all the details of the lives of those involved. It is a remarkable statement that is made, time and time again, of how God led. Even in this early day, there were those in that social climate who were looking to God and following His leading. Some would have us believe that this took place in the Stone Age, when man was a caveman and pretty much uncivilized. Don't believe a word of it! Here is a record that shows that man did not start out as that kind of man at all—and we find here the leading of God. If God could lead in the lives of these folk, He can lead in your life and my life. The second thing to notice in this chapter is the straightforward manner in which Rebekah made her decision to go with the servant and become the bride of Isaac. This is a tremendous thing which we will notice as we go through.

And Abraham was old, and well stricken in age: and the Lord had blessed Abraham in all things [Gen. 24:1].

Abraham is old, well stricken in age, and the Lord has blessed him in all things. Abraham now wants to get a bride for his son Isaac, but he does not want to get a bride among the Canaanites where the people are given to idolatry and paganism, and so he will send his servant to his people, back in the land of Haran, to get a bride for Isaac.

And Abraham said unto his eldest servant of his house, that ruled over all that he had, Put, I pray thee, thy hand under my thigh [Gen. 24:2].

This is the way men took an oath in that day. They did not raise their right hands and put their left hands on a Bible. They didn't have a Bible to begin with, and frankly, I do not think it is necessary for anyone to put his hand on a Bible to swear that he is telling the truth. If he intends to lie, he will lie even if his hand is resting on a Bible. The method in that day was for a man to put his hand under the thigh of the man to whom he was going to make an oath. I think this servant was Eliezer. He was the head servant in the home of Abraham, and he had a son—remember that Abraham had called God's attention to that earlier (see Gen. 15:2–3).

> **And I will make thee swear by the LORD, the God of heaven, and the God of the earth, that thou shalt not take a wife unto my son of the daughters of the Canaanites, among whom I dwell [Gen. 24:3].**

My Christian friend, if you have a boy or girl in your home who is marriageable, you ought to pray that he will not marry one of the "Canaanites." They are still in the land, and there is always a danger of our young people marrying one of them. If they do, as someone has put it, they are going to have the devil for their father-in-law, and they are always going to have trouble with him.

> **But thou shalt go unto my country, and to my kindred, and take a wife unto my son Isaac.**
>
> **And the servant said unto him, Peradventure the woman will not be willing to follow me unto this land: must I needs bring thy son again unto the land from whence thou camest?**
>
> **And Abraham said unto him, Beware thou that thou bring not my son thither again [Gen. 24:4–6].**

In other words the servant says to Abraham, "Suppose I cannot find a girl who will come with me. Shall I come back and get Isaac to take him to that land?" And Abraham says, "Never take Isaac back! This is the place where God wants us. Do not return him to that land under any circumstances." This is very important for us to see.

The LORD God of heaven, which took me from my father's house, and from the land of my kindred, and which spake unto me, and that sware unto me, saying, Unto thy seed will I give this land; he shall send his angel before thee, and thou shalt take a wife unto my son from thence [Gen. 24:7].

Abraham is really a man of faith. He demonstrates it again and again, and here he is magnificent. He says to this servant, "You can count on God to lead you. God has promised me this." Abraham is not taking a leap in the dark—*faith* is not a leap in the dark. It must rest upon the Word of God. Many people say, "I believe God, and it will come to pass." That's fine. It is wonderful for you to believe God, but do you have something in writing from Him? Abraham always asked for it in writing, and he had it in writing from God. God had made a contract with him. Abraham is really saying, "God has promised me that through my seed Isaac He is going to bring a blessing to the world. You can be sure of one thing: God has a bride back there for Isaac." You see, Abraham rests upon what God has said. We need to not be foolish today. Faith is not foolishness. It is resting upon something. It is always reasonable. It is never a leap in the dark. It is not betting your life that this or that will come to pass. It is not a gamble; it is a sure thing. Faith is the real sure thing. Abraham is sure.

And if the woman will not be willing to follow thee, then thou shalt be clear from this my oath: only bring not my son thither again [Gen. 24:8].

Abraham says, "Don't ever take my son back there, but if the woman won't come, then you are discharged." What does that mean? I think it means simply that Abraham would have told you, "God has another way of working this out. I don't know what it will be, but I am very sure that God does not want my son to marry a godless girl"

My friend, that is what faith is. Faith is acting upon the Word of God. Faith rests upon something. God wants us to believe His Word and not just believe. It is pious nonsense to think that you can force God to do something, that God has to do it because you believe it. I have made it through a number of years now with cancer in my body, and no one wants to be healed more than I do. Don't tell me that I don't believe in faith healing—I do. However, I have been told that I can force God, that God *will* heal me if I demand it. I do not know what His will is, but whatever His will is, that is what I want done. God wants us to bring our needs to Him, but He has to be the One to determine how He will answer our prayers. Abraham has something to rest upon. He is not demanding anything of God. He says, "If this doesn't work out, then God has another way to work it out."

And the servant put his hand under the thigh of Abraham his master, and sware to him concerning that matter [Gen. 24:9].

Now watch the servant as he goes out to get a bride for Isaac.

And the servant took ten camels of the camels of his master, and departed; for all the goods of his master were in his hand: and he arose, and went to Mesopotamia, unto the city of Nahor [Gen. 24:10].

The servant who is going to Mesopotamia to get a bride for Isaac takes ten camels along, and that means somebody had to ride them. He took along quite a retinue of servants.

"For all the goods of his master were in his hand." In other words, he had charge of all the chattels and all the possessions of Abraham.

And he made his camels to kneel down without the city by a well of water at the time of the evening, even the time that women go out to draw water [Gen. 24:11].

It may seem strange to you that the women came out to draw water, but they were the ones who did the watering of the camels in that day. Very frankly, women did lots more work in those days than they do today— I mean by that, *hard* physical labor. The women were the ones who watered and took care of the stock. The men were supposed to be out trading and doing other work—they were not always loafing, by any means. But it is interesting to note that it was the custom of that day for women to go out to draw water. This servant was waiting because it was not the proper thing for him, as a stranger, to water his camels before the others who lived in that community.

This servant is depending upon God. Abraham had put all of this in the hands of the Lord, and now the servant does also:

And he said, O Lord God of my master Abraham, I pray thee, send me good speed this day, and shew kindness unto my master Abraham.

Behold, I stand here by the well of water; and the daughters of the men of the city come out to draw water:

And let it come to pass, that the damsel to whom I shall say, Let down thy pitcher, I pray thee, that I may drink; and she shall say, Drink, and I will give thy camels drink also: let the same be she that thou hast appointed for thy servant Isaac; and thereby shall I know that thou hast shewed kindness unto my master [Gen. 24:12–14].

The servant's prayer is something like this: "The daughters of the men of the city will be coming out. I do not know which one to choose, and it is just left up to me to pick one of them. I pray that the one that I pick might be the one that You pick." In other words, he calls upon the Lord to lead him in making the right choice.

Who do you think he is going to pick? Well, he is a man, and he is going to pick the best looking woman who comes out. And you can be sure of one thing—Rebekah was a good looking woman. The Puritans had the idea that beauty was of the devil. The devil *is* beautiful—he's an angel of light, by the way—but he does not have it all. After all, God is the Creator, and you have never seen a sunset or looked at a beautiful flower that He did not make. He makes women beautiful, and there is nothing wrong with that. I am sure this man is going to pick the best looking one who comes out—he'd be a pretty poor servant if he didn't.

> **And it came to pass, before he had done speaking, that, behold, Rebekah came out, who was born to Bethuel, son of Milcah, the wife of Nahor, Abraham's brother, with her pitcher upon her shoulder.**

> **And the damsel was very fair to look upon, a virgin, neither had any man known her: and she went down to the well, and filled her pitcher, and came up [Gen. 24:15–16].**

I told you Rebekah was good looking—I knew it was coming, of course. She was good looking—the Word of God says it, my friend, and there is nothing wrong with that. I resent it today that Hollywood, the theater, and the devil get beauty. I think that the Lord ought to have some of it. He made it to begin with, and there is nothing wrong with His using a lovely and beautiful person. I pray always that God will call fine looking men and women into His service today.

"And the damsel was very fair to look upon." She was not just an ordinary girl. She would have won a beauty contest. She was "a virgin, neither had any man known her."

> **And the servant ran to meet her, and said, Let me, I pray thee, drink a little water of thy pitcher.**

> **And she said, Drink, my lord: and she hasted, and let down her pitcher upon her hand, and gave him drink.**

> **And when she had done giving him drink, she said, I will draw water for thy camels also, until they have done drinking [Gen. 24:17–19].**

The important thing to note is that Rebekah is a very polite and courteous girl also. She is beautiful, not dumb, and very polite.

And she hasted, and emptied her pitcher into the trough, and ran again unto the well to draw water, and drew for all his camels [Gen. 24:20].

Remember that there were ten camels, and I do not know how long it had been since they had last filled their tanks. It was just like filling the radiator of a car to fill up those camels.

And the man wondering at her held his peace, to wit whether the LORD had made his journey prosperous or not [Gen. 24:21].

The servant just stands there in amazement. He is wondering whether this is it, whether God is leading or not—he believes He is.

And it came to pass, as the camels had done drinking, that the man took a golden earring of half a shekel weight, and two bracelets for her hands of ten shekels weight of gold;

And said, Whose daughter art thou? tell me, I pray thee: is there room in thy father's house for us to lodge in?

And she said unto him, I am the daughter of Bethuel the son of Milcah, which she bare unto Nahor [Gen. 24:22–24].

Nahor is a brother of Abraham.

She said moreover unto him, We have both straw and provender enough, and room to lodge in.

And the man bowed down his head, and worshipped the LORD [Gen. 24:25–26].

The servant sees the hand of God in this. It is wonderful to have God leading and guiding, is it not?

And he said, Blessed be the LORD God of my master Abraham, who hath not left destitute my master of his mercy and his truth: I being in the way, the LORD led me to the house of my master's brethren [Gen. 24:27].

This is a great statement here: "I being in the way, the LORD led me. . . ." The Lord leads those who are in the way—that is, those who are in *His* way, who are wanting to be led, who will be led of Him, and who will do what He wants done. God can lead a willing heart anytime.

And the damsel ran, and told them of her mother's house these things.

And Rebekah had a brother, and his name was Laban: and Laban ran out unto the man, unto the well [Gen. 24:28–29].

Right here, let me warn you to keep your eye on Uncle Laban. He will bear watching at this point and from here on. He was greatly impressed by material things. Notice what happens:

And it came to pass, when he saw the earring and bracelets upon his sister's hands, and when he heard the words of Rebekah his sister, saying, Thus spake the man unto me; that he came unto the man; and, behold, he stood by the camels at the well [Gen. 24:30].

The servant just waited out there at the well to see whether anyone would come out to lead him into the home of Rebekah, whether he really had a welcome or not. Believe me, when old Laban saw those rings, he knew it was a very wealthy guest. Uncle Laban is not one to miss a deal. (If you doubt that, ask Jacob later on. Jacob found out that

Uncle Laban was a real trader; in fact, he was a better trader than Jacob was.) So Laban went out to welcome the servant.

And he said, Come in, thou blessed of the LORD; wherefore standest thou without? for I have prepared the house, and room for the camels [Gen. 24:31].

Even old Laban recognized the fact that there was the living God, the Creator, the one God.

And the man came into the house: and he ungirded his camels, and gave straw and provender for the camels, and water to wash his feet, and the men's feet that were with him [Gen. 24:32].

Again, we have this footwashing ceremony. Note that there are quite a few men who have come with this servant. The servant is entertained royally in this home—Uncle Laban sees to that.

We have here a marvelous picture of the relationship of Christ and the church. One of the figures of speech that is used in the New Testament is that the church is someday to become the bride of Christ. This is the way the church is being won today, through the Holy Spirit whom the Father and the Son have sent into the world. The Spirit of God, like the servant of Abraham, has come to talk about Another, to take the things of Christ and show them unto us. As this servant has gone to get a bride for Isaac, so the Spirit of God is in the world to call out a bride for Christ. Notice the marvelous dramatic effect that we have here. This is an exciting story and a wonderful record of that day.

And there was set meat before him to eat: but he said, I will not eat, until I have told mine errand. And he said, Speak on [Gen. 24:33].

Abraham's servant says, "Before I can eat, I want to tell you my mission." This is also characteristic of the Holy Spirit who has come into the world to tell about Another. That is primary business as far as God is concerned. I know that there are other businesses that are very important: the business of our government, the great business of the news media, and the great corporations, the automobile and the airplane companies. All this is important, great business. But ⌐od is not continuing to deal with this world because of General Motors or the government in Washington, D.C. (whether Republican or Democrat). The stock market on Wall Street is of no great concern in heaven. The thing that is primary as far as God is concerned is to get the gospel out to the peoples of the world. The Spirit of God is here to put this first. The servant of Abraham will not eat before he has spoken, and so they tell him to speak on.

And he said, I am Abraham's servant [Gen. 24:34].

Notice that his name is not given. Likewise, the Lord Jesus said that when the Holy Spirit comes, He will not speak of Himself, but He will take the things of Mine and show them unto you (see John 16:13–15). By the way, what is the name of the Holy Spirit? He has no name. He does not come to speak of Himself; He has come to speak of Another, of Christ. Similarly, this servant is not named but is simply called a servant of Abraham.

And the LORD hath blessed my master greatly; and he is become great: and he hath given him flocks, and herds, and silver, and gold, and menservants, and maidservants, and camels, and asses [Gen. 24:35].

The servant tells about the father's house. And that is something that the Spirit of God would have us know about. He convicts the world of sin, righteousness, and judgment—those are the three things that He talks about to the lost world. He would have us know that the judgment is upon a sinful earth and upon mankind. Men are lost today because they are sinners. I hear it said that men are lost because they reject Christ. They are *not* lost because they reject Christ; they are lost because they are sinners. Whether they have heard about Him or not, they are lost sinners. That is the condition of man today. The Holy Spirit has come to let us know that there is a Savior who has borne our judgment and who has been made over to us righteousness and that we can have a standing in heaven. The Holy Spirit has come to speak of Another.

"And the LORD hath blessed my master greatly." And, my friend, our Heavenly Father is rich today in cattle and in goods. The cattle on a thousand hills are His. How great our Father is!

And Sarah my master's wife bare a son to my master when she was old: and unto him hath he given all that he hath [Gen. 24:36].

In an infinitely greater way, the Lord Jesus is the Inheritor, and we are joint heirs with Him today. The servant of Abraham has come to tell this family that he is after a bride for his master's son who is going to inherit all things.

And my master made me swear, saying, Thou shalt not take a wife to my son of the daughters of the Canaanites, in whose land I dwell [Gen. 24:37].

The Holy Spirit is calling out sinners, but they are sinners who are ". . . born again, not of corruptible seed, but of incorruptible, by the word of God, which liveth and abideth for ever" (1 Pet. 1:23). These are the ones He is calling out—yes, sinners—but they have been made children of God. ". . . If any man be in Christ, he is a new creature . . ." (2 Cor. 5:17). God is not taking "Canaanites"; His children must be transformed.

But thou shalt go unto my father's house, and to my kindred, and take a wife unto my son.

And I said unto my master, Peradventure the woman will not follow me.

And he said unto me, The LORD, before whom I walk, will send his angel with thee, and prosper thy way; and thou shalt take a wife for my son of my kindred, and of my father's house:

Then shalt thou be clear from this my oath, when thou comest to my kindred; and if they give not thee one, thou shalt be clear from my oath.

And I came this day unto the well, and said, O LORD God of my master Abraham, if now thou do prosper my way which I go:

Behold, I stand by the well of water; and it shall come to pass, that when the virgin cometh forth to draw water, and I say to her, Give me, I pray thee, a little water of thy pitcher to drink;

And she say to me, Both drink thou, and I will also draw for thy camels: let the same be the woman whom the LORD hath appointed out for my master's son.

And before I had done speaking in mine heart, behold, Rebekah came forth with her pitcher on her shoulder; and she went down unto the well, and drew water: and I said unto her, Let me drink, I pray thee.

And she made haste, and let down her pitcher from her shoulder, and said, Drink, and I will give thy camels drink also: so I drank, and she made the camels drink also.

And I asked her, and said, Whose daughter art thou? And she said, The daughter of Bethuel, Nahor's son, whom Milcah bare unto him: and I put the earring upon her face, and the bracelets upon her hands.

And I bowed down my head, and worshipped the LORD, and blessed the LORD God of my master Abraham,

> which had led me in the right way to take my master's brother's daughter unto his son.
>
> And now if ye will deal kindly and truly with my master, tell me: and if not, tell me; that I may turn to the right hand, or to the left [Gen. 24:38–49].

Laban is the spokesman for this family. Listen to him:

> Then Laban and Bethuel answered and said, The thing proceedeth from the LORD: we cannot speak unto thee bad or good.
>
> Behold, Rebekah is before thee, take her and go, and let her be thy master's son's wife, as the LORD hath spoken [Gen. 24:50–51].

They say, "As far as we are concerned, this is of the Lord. You go ahead and take Rebekah."

> And it came to pass, that, when Abraham's servant heard their words, he worshipped the LORD, bowing himself to the earth.
>
> And the servant brought forth jewels of silver, and jewels of gold, and raiment, and gave them to Rebekah: he gave also to her brother and to her mother precious things [Gen. 24:52–53].

This is the way the Spirit gives to the children of God. We have the earnest, the guarantee, of the Spirit when we come to Christ. Being justified by faith, we have peace with God, we have access, we have joy, we have a hope, and we have the Holy Spirit (see Rom. 5:1–5). These are the wonderful things that have been made over to the believer today.

> And they did eat and drink, he and the men that were
> with him, and tarried all night; and they rose up in the
> morning, and he said, Send me away unto my master.

> And her brother and her mother said, Let the damsel
> abide with us a few days, at the least ten; after that she
> shall go [Gen. 24:54–55].

The very next morning this servant says, "I want to be on my way." I'll
tell you, this is big business for him! And the brother says, "What's
your hurry? Give us at least ten days to tell her good-bye. After all, we
had better talk this over with her."

> And he said unto them, Hinder me not, seeing the LORD
> hath prospered my way; send me away that I may go to
> my master.

> And they said, We will call the damsel, and inquire at
> her mouth [Gen. 24:56–57].

We have come to this very important part that I think is quite wonderful. Don't miss this.

> And they called Rebekah, and said unto her, Wilt thou
> go with this man? And she said, I will go [Gen. 24:58].

Let's take another look at this picture. It is an oriental scene, couched
way back yonder in the beginning of time, at the dawn of humanity, in
a way. Although I am confident that man had been on this earth thou-
sands of years at this time, as far as we are concerned, this was ap-
proximately four thousand years ago. This family is entertaining a
guest, a stranger, and they are entertaining him royally. They have fed
his camels and taken care of the servants. They have set meat before
him, a real feast, but he wanted to state his business.

And so he tells his strange business. He has come to get a bride for
his master's son, Isaac. I can see this servant as he brings out the gifts

to give to this family—gold and silver trinkets. Abraham, you must remember, was a very rich man. Then the servant begins to tell about the master. As he speaks, I see that family circle around the fire, and in the background, standing just beyond the others, I see a very beautiful girl with deep brown eyes. She is listening intently. She hears the servant tell about Abraham and about how Isaac was born. The servant tells about Isaac's miraculous birth and about his life. Then he tells about the day that his father took him yonder to the top of Mount Moriah to offer him as a sacrifice and how God spared him and would not take his life but gave him back to the father alive. And finally he tells how the father has sent him, a servant, to get a bride for Isaac. They do not want to get a bride for him from among the Canaanites. They must get one who is of like mind, one who has the same capacity for the living God, one who is born again of the Word of God. He is looking for a bride.

Rebekah has been listening all this time, and now they turn to her. No one has paid much attention to her up to this point, but now all eyes turn to her, and they say, "Rebekah, what about it? Will you go with this man?" She does not hedge or fudge or beat around the bush or hesitate. She says, *"I will go."*

Have you ever noticed that the men whom the Lord Jesus called as His disciples made the same instant decision? They left their nets and followed Him. Oh, I know that they went back a couple of times, but there came a day when they broke loose from those nets, and they never went back to them. They followed Him; they went with Him. The Holy Spirit is still calling today. He is the One who has taken the servant's place. You see, the Father and the Spirit sent the Son into the world to die for the world. And when the Son went back to heaven, He said He would send the Holy Spirit, the Comforter. The Spirit has now come into the world, and He is calling out a bride. He is saying, "Will you go? Here is the One who died for you. He will save you. You have to be redeemed first. You have to come as a sinner to Him, take your rightful position, and accept Him as Savior. When you do, you will be born again; you will become a child of God and be put into the church that is going to be presented to Him someday as a bride." The question is: Will you go? Will you accept the invitation? Will you trust

Christ as your Savior? This is not something about which you can beat around the bush—you either do it or you don't.

I never shall forget the time that I was speaking in a certain place in Texas. I presented Christ, and then I asked, "Will you accept Him?" I really wasn't through preaching, but I never shall forget a young man who sat there, and I could tell he was interested. He got up right there and then and walked down. It had a tremendous effect upon the audience. He was not wishywashy; there wasn't anything uncertain about him. My, I love a clean-cut decision like that! That is the way He wants you, my friend. That is the way He will accept you, and it is the only way He will accept you.

This does not end the story. They start out now, and they are going back to the Promised Land.

> **And they sent away Rebekah their sister, and her nurse, and Abraham's servant, and his men.**

> **And they blessed Rebekah, and said unto her, Thou art our sister, be thou the mother of thousands of millions, and let thy seed possess the gate of those which hate them [Gen. 24:59-60].**

This prophecy has already been fulfilled. We are not talking here about unfulfilled, but fulfilled, prophecy.

> **And Rebekah arose, and her damsels, and they rode upon the camels, and followed the man: and the servant took Rebekah, and went his way [Gen. 24:61].**

They had a long trip back. We are not told anything about this trip, but I know that it is not easy riding a camel. I rode one from the little village outside of Cairo down to the pyramids—and that's as far as I want to ride on a camel! They call them "the ships of the desert." Well, it was as rough as any trip I have ever had on a boat. It was rough! They are not easy to ride, but imagine riding on those camels across the desert. I can see them after a hard day on that hot desert. At evening they stop at an oasis, the campfire is built, and they have their evening meal. As they are sitting there before going to bed to get their sleep, I hear Rebekah say to this servant, "Tell me about Isaac again." The servant says, "What do you want me to tell you?" She says, "Tell me about the way he was born. Tell me about the way his father offered him on the altar." It was like our song, "Tell me the old, old story of Jesus and His love!" And the servant says, "I told you that last night." Rebekah says, "I know, but tell it again. Tell it again." And so the servant tells it again. It never grows old. That night Rebekah has that sweet sleep, dreaming of the time when she will meet this one. The next day they start out on the journey again, and the desert isn't quite as hot, and the camel isn't quite as rough. But it is a long ways, and so they continue until they finally come in sight of the land of promise. They enter it and come down to Lahai-roi.

And Isaac came from the way of the well Lahai-roi; for he dwelt in the south country [Gen. 24:62].

This is way down in the pleasant country of Hebron and Beer-sheba.

And Isaac went out to meditate in the field at the eventide: and he lifted up his eyes, and saw, and, behold, the camels were coming [Gen. 24:63].

In this human episode, we are given a view of the coming of Christ for His bride. Many people are saying, "Won't it be wonderful when the Lord comes and we will be caught up with Him?" There is another view, and that is of those who will be with Him when He comes. Most of the church has already gone through the doorway of death, and they will be coming with Him when He comes. Their bodies will be raised and their spirits and bodies joined together. Those who are alive are to be caught up with the dead to meet the Lord in the air. Those who have gone before in death are going to see Him when He arises from the right hand of the Father and starts out to call His church to meet Him in the air. This is the picture, and what a glorious picture it is!

And Rebekah lifted up her eyes, and when she saw
Isaac, she lighted off the camel.

For she had said unto the servant, What man is this that
walketh in the field to meet us? And the servant had
said, It is my master: therefore she took a veil, and covered herself [Gen. 24:64–65].

We as the bride of Christ will have to be clothed with the righteousness of Christ, but He has been made over to us righteousness. He was
delivered for our offenses, and He was raised for our justification in
order that we might have a righteousness which will enable us to
stand before God.

Rebekah, seeing a man walking toward them, asks who he is.
Throughout the long journey she has come to know *about* him, but
now she is to see him face to face. This is similar to our position even
now. As Peter expressed it, "Whom having not seen, ye love . . ."
(1 Peter 1:8). I wonder: When He does come, are we going to know
Him? In a song there are these words: "I shall know Him, I shall know
Him by the prints of the nails in His hands." I think this is the way that
we are going to know Him when He comes. What a glorious, wonderful, beautiful picture we have before us!

**And the servant told Isaac all things that he had done
[Gen. 24:66].**

The Holy Spirit has sealed us and will deliver us to Christ at the day of
redemption. Believe me, it was certain that this servant of Abraham's
was going to get the bride to Isaac.

Now this is the union of Isaac and Rebekah—

And Isaac brought her into his mother Sarah's tent, and
took Rebekah, and she became his wife; and he loved
her: and Isaac was comforted after his mother's death
[Gen. 24:67].

"And he loved her"—Christ loved the church and gave Himself for her. "And Isaac was comforted after his mother's death." This reveals to us that Christ gains a great deal in our salvation. He wants us; He longs for us. Oh, that you and I might be faithful to Him, my beloved!

CHAPTER 25

THEME: Abraham marries Keturah; Abraham dies; Esau and Jacob

This is another great chapter of the Bible. It records the death of Abraham and the birth of the twins, Esau and Jacob, to Isaac and Rebekah. It gives the generations of Ishmael and also the generations of Isaac. Then there is the incident relative to the birthright. So this is a remarkable chapter, and it covers a great deal of ground.

This chapter concludes the account of Abraham's life, but, frankly, his story ended back in chapter 23 when he sent the servant out to get a bride for Isaac.

ABRAHAM MARRIES KETURAH

Then again Abraham took a wife, and her name was Keturah.

And she bare him Zimran, and Jokshan, and Medan, and Midian, and Ishbak, and Shuah [Gen. 25:1–2].

Now he has quite a family. He had his biggest family after the death of Sarah. Somebody will raise the question, "I thought that at the time of the birth of Isaac Abraham was dead as far as his capability of bringing a child into the world." Granted, he was. But when God does something, He really does it. This is the reason I believe that anything God does bears His signature. Right here we see that this man Abraham was not only able to bring Isaac into the world, but he now brings in this great family of children.

The interesting thing that we have before us here is the mention of Medan and Midian. The other boys will have nations come from them also, but I can't identify them. I'm not interested in them because they do not cross our pathway in Scripture, but Midian does. We will find later that Moses will go down into the land of Midian and take a wife from there. Remember that the Midianites are in the line of Abraham and so are the Medanites. So we find here the fact that there are other sons of Abraham, but the Lord has said it is through Isaac that Abraham's seed is called—not through any of these other sons. It is not through Ishmael, nor through Midian, nor Medan. All of these were nomads of the desert.

ABRAHAM DIES

And Abraham gave all that he had unto Isaac.

But unto the sons of the concubines, which Abraham had, Abraham gave gifts, and sent them away from Isaac his son, while he yet lived, eastward, unto the east country.

And these are the days of the years of Abraham's life which he lived, an hundred threescore and fifteen years.

Then Abraham gave up the ghost, and died in a good old age, an old man, and full of years; and was gathered to his people.

And his sons Isaac and Ishmael buried him in the cave of Machpelah, in the field of Ephron the son of Zohar the Hittite, which is before Mamre;

The field which Abraham purchased of the sons of Heth: there was Abraham buried, and Sarah his wife [Gen. 25:5–10].

Ishmael comes for the funeral because, after all, Abraham is his father. So Isaac and Ishmael together bury Abraham. Then Isaac goes down to live at the place where he first met Rebekah.

And it came to pass after the death of Abraham, that God blessed his son Isaac; and Isaac dwelt by the well Lahai-roi [Gen. 25:11].

In verses 12 to 18 we have the generations of Ishmael, Abraham's son, whom Hagar the Egyptian, Sarah's handmaid, bare unto Abraham. The list of them is given here. I call to your attention again the fact that the Holy Spirit uses this method in the Book of Genesis. The rejected line is given first and then set aside and not mentioned anymore. Then the line that is leading to Christ is given and followed. So it is after the line of Ishmael is given that we come to the line of Isaac.

ESAU AND JACOB

And these are the generations of Isaac, Abraham's son: Abraham begat Isaac [Gen. 25:19].

This is the line we are going to follow. "Abraham begat Isaac; and Isaac begat Jacob" is the way the first chapter of Matthew begins. Each of these men had other sons, as we have seen. Abraham had quite a few sons, but the genealogy of those men is not followed. It is the genealogy of Isaac that is followed. You can forget Ishmael and Midian and Medan and all the rest. They will cross paths with the descendants of Isaac time and again, but we will not follow their lines.

> **And Isaac was forty years old when he took Rebekah to wife, the daughter of Bethuel the Syrian of Padan-aram, the sister to Laban the Syrian.**
>
> **And Isaac entreated the LORD for his wife, because she was barren: and the LORD was entreated of him, and Rebekah his wife conceived [Gen. 25:20–21].**

It is interesting that Rebekah, like Sarah, was barren. But Isaac pled with God on her behalf, and now she is pregnant with twins.

> And the children struggled together within her; and she
> said, If it be so, why am I thus? And she went to inquire
> of the LORD [Gen. 25:22].

The struggle of these two boys, which began before their birth, represents *the* struggle which still goes on in the world today. There is a struggle between light and darkness, between good and evil, between the Spirit and the flesh. Every child of God knows something of this struggle which Paul sets before us in the seventh chapter of Romans.

Rebekah didn't understand the struggle which was going on within her, and she went to the Lord with the question, "Why am I thus?"

> And the LORD said unto her, Two nations are in thy
> womb, and two manner of people shall be separated
> from thy bowels; and the one people shall be stronger
> than the other people; and the elder shall serve the
> younger [Gen. 25:23].

God makes the statement to her that the elder shall serve the younger. She should have believed it, and her younger son should have believed it.

> And when her days to be delivered were fulfilled, behold, there were twins in her womb.

> And the first came out red, all over like an hairy garment; and they called his name Esau [Gen. 25:24–25].

The name *Esau* means "red" or "earth-colored." Because he is born first, he is considered the elder. But the elder is to serve the younger.

> And after that came his brother out, and his hand took
> hold on Esau's heel; and his name was called Jacob: and
> Isaac was threescore years old when she bare them
> [Gen. 25:26].

Isaac and Rebekah had been married for about twenty years before the children were born. The older one was Esau, and they called him "Red," if you please. Jacob took hold on Esau's heel; so they called him Jacob, meaning the usurper, because he was trying to become the elder or to take his place—but God had already promised that to him.

And the boys grew: and Esau was a cunning hunter, a man of the field; and Jacob was a plain man, dwelling in tents [Gen. 25:27].

Now we will look at these two boys as they grow up in this home. Here they are, twins, but no two boys were ever more different than these two. They not only struggled in the womb, but they are against each other from here on out. They have absolutely different viewpoints, different philosophies of life. Their thinking is different, and their attitudes are different. At the beginning, I must confess, Esau is more attractive than Jacob. But we learn that one can't always judge by the outward sign. We must judge by what takes place on the inside. We learn that in this particular case.

"The boys grew." This fellow Esau was a cunning hunter, the outdoor boy, the athletic type. He is the one we would call the all-American boy today. He went in for sports. He went in for everything that was physical, but he had no understanding or capacity or desire for spiritual things. He was only interested in that which was physical. He represents the flesh.

Jacob was a plain man. I think that you can make of that anything you want to. He lived indoors. He was mama's boy and was tied to her apron strings. You will notice that he did what she told him to do. Jacob is really a mama's boy.

And this boy Esau is papa's boy—

And Isaac loved Esau, because he did eat of his venison: but Rebekah loved Jacob [Gen. 25:28].

Here is the problem in the home. You feel that under these circumstances they are going to have trouble, and they are. When one parent is partial to one child and the other parent is partial to the other child, you have trouble. That is exactly what took place here.

Isaac loved him because he ate of his venison. Esau went out hunting, and he always got something when he went hunting. He brought home the venison. Isaac liked that, and he liked this outdoor type of boy. Rebekah loved Jacob because he was a mama's boy.

As I have said before, at this juncture the boy Esau is much more attractive than Jacob. He seems to be a more wholesome boy. The boy Jacob is cunning; he tries to be clever. The fact of the matter is that he doesn't mind stooping to do things that are absolutely wrong. (And God will deal with him for this.) The interesting thing is that although Esau was very attractive on the outside, down underneath he really had no capacity for God whatever. If ever there was a man of the world, he is that man. He is just a physical man and that is all. That is all that he lived for.

Down underneath in Jacob there was a desire for the things that are spiritual. It took God a long time to rub off all the debris that was on top and to remove all the coverings in order to get down to where the spiritual desire was, but He finally did it. Before we are through with our study of Jacob (and his story goes almost all the way through the Book of Genesis), we will see that he was God's man all along, although he didn't demonstrate it until late in life.

Now we are told of an incident which took place in the home. You can well understand that the partiality shown by both father and mother would cause difficulty and conflict. It could not be called a happy home.

And Jacob sod pottage: and Esau came from the field, and he was faint:

And Esau said to Jacob, Feed me, I pray thee, with that same red pottage; for I am faint: therefore was his name called Edom.

And Jacob said, Sell me this day thy birthright.

And Esau said, Behold, I am at the point to die: and
what profit shall this birthright do to me? [Gen. 25:29–
32].

This incident reveals the nature of both of these men. Esau came from
the field. He had been outdoors, and he was tired. He was not starving
to death as some would imply. No one who had been brought up in the
home of Abraham would starve to death. There would always be
something for him to eat. The thing was that there was nothing prepared right at that moment but this pottage, this stew, which Jacob had
made. Jacob was the indoor boy. Evidently he was a good chef.

"Feed me, I pray thee, with that same red (notice in your King
James Version that the word *pottage* is in italics, meaning that the
word has been supplied by the translators); for I am faint: therefore
was his name called Edom." *Edom* means red or earthy just as *Esau*
does. This man asks for some of the stew, and Jacob saw his chance.
He is a trickster and a traitor, and he wanted the birthright. He said,
"Sell me this day thy birthright."

Let's stop and look for a minute at the value of the birthright and
what it means. It means that the one who had it was the head of the
house. It also means that the one who had it was the priest of the family. In this particular family, it means that the one who had it would be
the one who would be in the line that would lead to Christ. Do you
think that Esau had valued it at all? Jacob knew that he didn't. He
attached no importance to it, and he didn't want to be the priest of the
family. In fact, that's the last thing that he wanted to be.

In our day, sometimes when a Christian is asked to do something
for the cause of Christ, he replies, "Oh, I'm not a preacher; I can't do
that!" There are too many folk today who do not *want* to do that which
is spiritual. They don't even want to give the impression that they are
interested in spiritual things.

That was Esau. He didn't want to give that impression. If anyone
would have called him "deacon" or "preacher," it would have insulted
him. He didn't want the birthright. He didn't care about being in the

line that led to Christ. No one could have cared less about being in that line.

Jacob sees this, and he says to him, "I'll tell you what I'll do, if you'll give me your birthright, I'll give you a bowl of stew." Esau was very happy with the bargain. He said, "I'll be very happy to do it; what profit is the birthright to me? What do I care about the birthright? I'd rather have a bowl of stew." That is the value which he attached to spiritual things.

Let us remember that Jacob also was wrong in what he did. God had promised, "The elder shall serve the younger." The birthright is coming to Jacob in God's own time. Jacob can't wait; so he reaches out to take that which God has promised him. He takes it in a clever, tricky fashion. He should have waited for God to give it to him.

This man operated on the principle that he would do what he could for himself. He thought that as long as he could help himself there was no reason to look to God to perform it. He felt thoroughly capable of taking care of his business. At the beginning he really did rather well as far as the world would measure him. But there came a day when God sent this man off to college, and Uncle Laban was the president of the college. It was known as the college of hard knocks, and Jacob was going to learn a few things in the college of hard knocks. But here he is still operating on the principle that he is clever enough to get what is coming to him.

And Jacob said, Swear to me this day; and he sware unto him: and he sold his birthright unto Jacob.

Then Jacob gave Esau bread and pottage of lentils; and he did eat and drink, and rose up, and went his way: thus Esau despised his birthright [Gen. 25:33–34].

"Esau *despised* his birthright" is the important thing to see at this juncture. So Esau sat down and ate his stew. He had surrendered his birthright because it meant nothing to him. Nothing that was spiritual meant anything to him. Unfortunately, I'm afraid we have church members like that. They have no spiritual capacity and no understanding of spiritual truths. I believe that the mark of a true Christian is one whom the Spirit of God can teach and guide. It is as if a man today had a very valuable heirloom, let's say an old family Bible which had belonged to his grandfather. Another grandson wants it and offers to give him a quarter for it. So the owner says, "Give me the twenty-five cents because I was going to throw the old thing away anyway." That is exactly what Esau would have done.

But Jacob is wrong also, and we'll see more of his cleverness and trickery in chapter 27.

CHAPTER 26

THEME: God reaffirms His covenant to Isaac; Isaac misrepresents Rebekah; Isaac in Gerar; Isaac goes to Beer-sheba

When I was a much younger preacher, this chapter did not seem to be very exciting. It is quite colorless and uninteresting, which is especially noticeable after we have studied a man like Abraham and an exciting man like Jacob who is to follow. This chapter is about Isaac. In fact, it is the only chapter that is really about Isaac, and it just isn't very thrilling. All he does is dig wells. However, in later years I've come to examine these chapters and have found that God has a message for us in this also. In fact, it is a very important message, and Paul stated it quite accurately: "For whatsoever things were written aforetime were written for our learning, that we through patience and comfort of the scriptures might have hope" (Rom. 15:4). This is a chapter that teaches patience, and some of us need that—certainly I am in that category. Yet, we would not have you get the impression that patience is all that God wants of us. The Lord also had men like Abraham, like Jacob, and like David, men who were real go-getters and who were aggressive. God can use that also. But the life of Isaac has a great message for many of us. "All scripture is given by inspiration of God, and is profitable for doctrine, for reproof, for correction, for instruction in righteousness: That the man of God may be perfect, throughly furnished unto all good works" (2 Tim. 3:16–17). With that in mind, let us come to this chapter.

Isaac, the beloved son, has the covenant confirmed to him. Then we find him dropping into the same sin of unbelief as his father Abraham had done. Finally, we see him digging wells in the land of Gerar. This doesn't seem to be very exciting but there is a message here for us; so let us not miss it.

GOD REAFFIRMS HIS COVENANT TO ISAAC

And there was a famine in the land, beside the first famine that was in the days of Abraham. And Isaac went unto Abimelech king of the Philistines unto Gerar [Gen. 26:1].

This is now the second famine that is mentioned. You remember the famine in the days of Abraham when Abraham and Lot took off for Egypt.

And the LORD appeared unto him, and said, Go not down into Egypt; dwell in the land which I shall tell thee of [Gen. 26:2].

Why did God say that to Isaac? Well, he had an example before him of his father who had run off down to the land of Egypt. This reveals the fact that "like father, like son," sins are carried from father to son. You can talk about the generation gap all you want, but there is no generation gap of sin. It just flows right from one generation to the other. Generally, the son makes very much the same mistakes that the father did, unless something intervenes.

So God gives definite instructions to Isaac at the time of famine. And He confirms the covenant which He had made with Abraham.

Sojourn in this land, and I will be with thee, and will bless thee; for unto thee, and unto thy seed, I will give all these countries, and I will perform the oath which I sware unto Abraham thy father;

And I will make thy seed to multiply as the stars of heaven, and will give unto thy seed all these countries; and in thy seed shall all the nations of the earth be blessed [Gen. 26:3–4].

God says to Isaac, "Don't leave this land, don't go down to Egypt. I want to confirm with *you* the covenant which I made with Abraham." And He repeats the threefold promise: (1) the *land*—"I will give unto thy seed all these countries"; (2) the *nation*—"I will make thy seed to multiply as the stars of heaven"; (3) the *blessing*—"and in thy seed shall all the nations of the earth be blessed."

> **Because that Abraham obeyed my voice, and kept my charge, my commandments, my statutes, and my laws [Gen. 26:5].**

At this point God had not yet given the Mosaic Law; Abraham was not under the Mosaic system. However, the important thing is that, when God told Abraham something, he *believed* God and *acted* upon it. He demonstrated his faith by action.

We have too many folk today who complain of a lack of reality in their Christian lives. A lady came in to talk to me some time ago who said that she believed but that she just couldn't be sure and that she didn't feel anything. Such uncertainty! I didn't have to talk to her long to find out that there was no action in her life. She was just sitting in the corner, twiddling her thumbs, saying, "I believe," and then expecting some great something to take place. That just doesn't happen. When you believe God, you act upon His promises. If you would call me right now to tell me that there is a certain amount of money in a bank in downtown Los Angeles and that you have put it in there for me and I should go down to get it, do you think I would just sit right here the rest of the day? My friend, if you know me, you would know that by the time you hung up the telephone I would have my hat on my head and I'd be going down there. Faith is what you act on. Faith is something that you step out on. Abraham believed God, and God counted it to him for righteousness. God is now telling Isaac that He wants him to be that same kind of man.

ISAAC MISREPRESENTS REBEKAH

And Isaac dwelt in Gerar [Gen. 26:6].

Gerar is to the south. Abraham and Isaac both lived in the southern part of that land. Actually, Abraham had come into the land up north to Shechem, but he ended up living down in the southern part at Hebron, the "place of communion."

> And the men of the place asked him of his wife; and he said, She is my sister: for he feared to say, She is my wife; lest, said he, the men of the place should kill me for Rebekah; because she was fair to look upon [Gen. 26:7].

Isaac is repeating the sin of his father. God had warned him not to go to Egypt; so he didn't go there but went to Gerar instead. In Gerar he must have seen the men casting glances toward Rebekah; so he says to her, "You tell them that you're my sister, not my wife." The difference between Abraham and Isaac is that Abraham told half a lie and Isaac told a whole lie. The one he is telling was cut out of the whole cloth.

> And it came to pass, when he had been there a long time, that Abimelech king of the Philistines looked out at a window, and saw, and, behold, Isaac was sporting with Rebekah his wife [Gen. 26:8].

I guess they were laughing and playing together.

> And Abimelech called Isaac, and said, Behold, of a surety she is thy wife: and how saidst thou, She is my sister? And Isaac said unto him, Because I said, Lest I die for her.

> And Abimelech said, What is this thou hast done unto us? one of the people might lightly have lien with thy wife, and thou shouldest have brought guiltiness upon us [Gen. 26:9-10].

Isaac had put these people in danger of committing a sin. Then Abimelech went on to say—

And Abimelech charged all his people, saying, He that toucheth this man or his wife shall surely be put to death [Gen. 26:11].

Abimelech became a very good friend of Isaac's. Isaac had the respect of the community just as Abraham had had. Both of them were outstanding men. I mention that here because from the rest of the chapter we might not get the impression that Isaac is an outstanding man.

ISAAC IN GERAR

Then Isaac sowed in that land, and received in the same year an hundredfold: and the LORD blessed him [Gen. 26:12].

God is with him, you see. That is the blessing that God promised to these people from the day He called Abraham. It was an earthly blessing. Later on when God put them into that land, He told them He would bless them in their basket; that is, it would be filled with foodstuff. God made that promise good when they were walking in fellowship with Him.

We must remember that He is not promising *us* that blessing. He has promised *spiritual* blessings to us. We are told that we are blessed with all spiritual blessings, and that is our portion today. But that blessing is on the same terms. It depends on our walk with God. If you will permit Him, He wants to bless you abundantly in your spiritual life. We find here that Isaac is greatly blessed—

And the man waxed great, and went forward, and grew until he became very great [Gen. 26:13].

Don't miss the fact that Isaac is greatly blessed. His field brings forth an *hundredfold!* The impression some of us have is that Abraham was outstanding, and Jacob was also, but not Isaac. Let me say that Isaac is also outstanding.

It is significant that the life of Isaac is tied in with that of Abraham. Isaac's birth and his life are interwoven with Abraham's experiences. Although Isaac was important when he was offered there upon the altar, again it was Abraham and Isaac together. Why should it be so presented? Well, we have already seen that all these things happened unto them for examples to us. It presents a wonderful picture of the intimacy between the Lord Jesus Christ and the Father. Jesus said, ". . . he that hath seen me hath seen the Father . . ." (John 14:9). And in the high priestly prayer of Jesus, He said, ". . . I have finished the work which thou gavest me to do" (John 17:4). Also, He said, ". . . My Father worketh hitherto, and I work" (John 5:17). Therefore, it is very proper that the story of Isaac and the story of Abraham be identified together.

Now here in the chapter before us we see Isaac standing on his own two feet, and he doesn't look too attractive. He exhibits a weakness and repeats the sin of Abraham. However, the Word of God makes it clear that Isaac was a very great man in that land—

For he had possession of flocks, and possession of herds, and great store of servants: and the Philistines envied him [Gen. 26:14].

The Philistines couldn't stand to see all this prosperity—

For all the wells which his father's servants had digged in the days of Abraham his father, the Philistines had stopped them, and filled them with earth [Gen. 26:15].

Abraham had been digging wells in that land, and now his son comes along and the wells become his. But he would go out in the morning and find that the wells were all filled up. This was done by the Philistines and, by the way, this is the first mention of the enmity of the Philistines. This led to continual warfare later on in the days of David.

> And Abimelech said unto Isaac, Go from us; for thou art
> much mightier than we [Gen. 26:16].

Notice the importance of Isaac at this time.

> And Isaac departed thence, and pitched his tent in the
> valley of Gerar, and dwelt there [Gen. 26:17].

This man Abimelech said, "You are causing a great deal of difficulty
now, and it would be better if you left." He had great respect for Isaac,
as you can see.

Now this is a part of Isaac's life that looks like weakness, but it is
not. Notice that he returns back to the land where his father Abraham
had been—

> And Isaac digged again the wells of water, which they
> had digged in the days of Abraham his father; for the
> Philistines had stopped them after the death of Abra-
> ham: and he called their names after the names by
> which his father had called them.
>
> And Isaac's servants digged in the valley, and found
> there a well of springing water.
>
> And the herdmen of Gerar did strive with Isaac's herd-
> men, saying, The water is ours: and he called the name
> of the well Esek; because they strove with him [Gen.
> 26:18–20].

This reveals the struggle that was carried on.

I feel that the water is a picture of the Word of God. We are to drink
deeply of it. It is called the "water of the Word" and is for drinking
purposes to slake our thirst, and it is also for washing. Jesus said that
we are cleansed through the Word which He has spoken.

Water is a very necessary item in life. You can't have life without
water. You can fly over the deserts of Arizona, New Mexico, and Cali-

fornia and see plenty of arid land. Then all of a sudden you see an area of lush green and wonder what has happened down there. Water is the only explanation.

And, my friend, water is the explanation for the differences between God's children in any church—the water of the Word of God. There is a great difference in the lives of believers who study God's Word. And there will be a struggle. I think that you will always have to pay a price if you are really going to study the Word of God. The devil will permit you to do anything except get into the Word of God.

> **And they digged another well, and strove for that also: and he called the name of it Sitnah.**

> **And he removed from thence, and digged another well; and for that they strove not: and he called the name of it Rehoboth; and he said, For now the Lord hath made room for us, and we shall be fruitful in the land [Gen. 26:21–22].**

Then he calls the well Rehoboth. It means "there is room for us." Before that he would dig a well and they would take it away from him. He'd move up, dig another one, and they would take that away from him. He would just keep moving up. This certainly reveals that Isaac is a man of peace and a man of patience. David wouldn't have done this, I can tell you that. Simon Peter wouldn't have done that. And if you want to know the truth, Vernon McGee wouldn't have done that. It is a real lesson for us here. This is especially applicable when we apply it to the study of the Word of God.

ISAAC GOES TO BEER-SHEBA

> **And he went up from thence to Beer-sheba.**

> **And the Lord appeared unto him the same night, and said, I am the God of Abraham thy father: fear not, for I am with thee, and will bless thee, and multiply thy seed for my servant Abraham's sake [Gen. 26:23–24].**

God appears to him to comfort him. God appeared to all the patriarchs with the exception of Joseph. He appeared to Abraham, Isaac,
and Jacob.

> **And he builded an altar there, and called upon the
> name of the LORD, and pitched his tent there: and there
> Isaac's servants digged a well [Gen. 26:25].**

He goes on again, digging wells. You can always put a well down next
to Isaac. You can put an altar down next to Abraham, and you can put
a tent down next to Jacob, as we shall see later on.

> **Then Abimelech went to him from Gerar, and Ahuzzath
> one of his friends, and Phichol the chief captain of his
> army.**
>
> **And Isaac said unto them, Wherefore come ye to me,
> seeing ye hate me, and have sent me away from you?**
>
> **And they said, We saw certainly that the LORD was with
> thee: and we said, Let there be now an oath betwixt us,
> even betwixt us and thee, and let us make a covenant
> with thee;**
>
> **That thou wilt do us no hurt, as we have not touched
> thee, and as we have done unto thee nothing but good,
> and have sent thee away in peace: thou art now the
> blessed of the LORD [Gen. 26:26–29].**

Although Isaac almost seems weak in his dealing with the men of
Gerar, the king of Gerar was so impressed that he followed Isaac to
Beer-sheba in order to establish good relations. The influence of Isaac
in that land was not that of a weak man.

> **And Esau was forty years old when he took to wife Ju-
> dith the daughter of Beeri the Hittite, and Bashemath
> the daughter of Elon the Hittite:**

Which were a grief of mind unto Isaac and to Rebekah [Gen. 26:34–35].

In the next chapter we will see Jacob in his true colors. Thereby hangs a tale.

CHAPTER 27

THEME: Jacob takes Esau's birthright; Jacob flees to Laban

This chapter has as its theme Jacob and Rebekah conniving to get the blessing of Isaac for Jacob. It is the blessing which Isaac intended for Esau. You see, Jacob wanted the blessing of his father. He knew God had promised his mother that the elder would serve the younger; so the blessing was his already. However, he did not believe God. Rebekah, his mother, did not believe God. Evidently Isaac, the father, didn't believe God or he would never have attempted to bypass Jacob and give the blessing to Esau. He followed his own feelings and appetite in contradiction to the distinct Word of God.

The method Jacob used in obtaining the birthright cannot be supported on any grounds whatsoever. He used fraud and deceit. His conduct was despicable. God did not condone this any more than He condoned the conduct of Sarah and Abraham in the matter of Hagar and Ishmael. God could not use the trickery and cleverness of Jacob. As we shall see, God deals with this man in a very definite way. Jacob had to pay for his sin in the same coin in which he sinned. You will note that as we get into this chapter.

Chapter 26 concluded with Esau, who was about forty years old, marrying two Hittite women. This was a grief to Isaac and to Rebekah. Now they recognize that, if Jacob is not to marry a Hittite or a Philistine, he must be sent away to Haran where Isaac got his bride from the family of Abraham.

JACOB TAKES ESAU'S BIRTHRIGHT

And it came to pass, that when Isaac was old, and his eyes were dim, so that he could not see, he called Esau his eldest son, and said unto him, My son: and he said unto him, Behold, here am I.

And he said, Behold now, I am old, I know not the day of my death:

Now therefore take, I pray thee, thy weapons, thy quiver and thy bow, and go out to the field, and take me some venison;

And make me savoury meat, such as I love, and bring it to me, that I may eat; that my soul may bless thee before I die [Gen. 27:1-4].

We have seen that Isaac was an outstanding man, a great man. Abimelech and the Philistines came to make a treaty with him since they feared him. He was patient and peace loving but also prominent and powerful. Here, however, he reveals that weakness of the flesh. All during his life, Esau had been his favorite while Jacob had been the favorite of Rebekah. Esau was the outdoor boy who would go out and bring in a deer or some other animal. He would barbecue it, and the old man would enjoy it. Now Isaac is very old and he wants to bless his favorite son. He knows very well that God has said the elder will serve the younger, but he bypasses that because he wants to bless Esau. So he tells Esau to go out and bring in some meat and he will bless him because of it. What a revelation this is of this family.

Have you noticed the family strife since we have come to this last major section of Genesis? There was strife in the family of Abraham because of Hagar. Now there is strife in this family over these twins.

And Rebekah heard when Isaac spake to Esau his son. And Esau went to the field to hunt for venison, and to bring it.

And Rebekah spake unto Jacob her son, saying, Behold, I heard thy father speak unto Esau thy brother, saying,

Bring me venison, and make me savoury meat, that I may eat, and bless thee before the LORD before my death.

Now therefore, my son, obey my voice according to that which I command thee [Gen. 27:5-8].

Rebekah overheard what Isaac said. Jacob is her favorite; so she conceives this deceitful plan. It is absolute trickery, and it cannot be condoned on any basis whatever. God is recording it as history, but He condemns it. We will see that. Remember the things that are being done here, and later you will see the chickens come home to roost for Jacob. Now Rebekah goes on to say to him:

> **Go now to the flock, and fetch me from thence two good kids of the goats; and I will make them savoury meat for thy father, such as he loveth:**

> **And thou shalt bring it to thy father, that he may eat, and that he may bless thee before his death.**

> **And Jacob said to Rebekah his mother, Behold, Esau my brother is a hairy man, and I am a smooth man [Gen. 27:9–11].**

Esau was not only an outdoor man and a red man, but he was also a hairy man.

> **My father peradventure will feel me, and I shall seem to him as a deceiver; and I shall bring a curse upon me, and not a blessing [Gen. 27:12].**

Not only will he *seem* to be a deceiver; he is a deceiver.

> **And his mother said unto him, Upon me be thy curse, my son; only obey my voice, and go fetch me them.**

> **And he went, and fetched, and brought them to his mother: and his mother made savoury meat, such as his father loved.**

> **And Rebekah took goodly raiment of her eldest son Esau, which were with her in the house, and put them upon Jacob her younger son:**

And she put the skins of the kids of the goats upon his
hands, and upon the smooth of his neck:

And she gave the savoury meat and the bread, which
she had prepared, into the hand of her son Jacob [Gen.
27:13–17].

My friend, I can't help but comment on this. She put that skin of the
kid of the goat on the back of his neck and on the back of his hands so
that when his father would feel him, he'd think it was Esau. She also
dressed him in Esau's clothes so he would smell like him! Apparently
the deodorant that Esau was using was not very potent. The fact of the
matter is, I think he was like the whimsical story I heard about two
men who were working in a very tight place. One of them finally said
to the other one, "Wow! I think the deodorant of one of us has quit
working." The other fellow answered, "It must be yours because I
don't use any!" Well, I don't think that Esau used any either, and I'm
not sure he had a shower very often. Even if you couldn't see him, you
could smell him.

And he came unto his father, and said, My father: and
he said, Here am I; who art thou, my son?

And Jacob said unto his father, I am Esau thy firstborn; I
have done according as thou badest me: arise, I pray
thee, sit and eat of my venison, that thy soul may bless
me.

And Isaac said unto his son, How is it that thou hast
found it so quickly, my son? And he said, Because the
LORD thy God brought it to me [Gen. 27:18–20].

Believe me, this boy at this particular point is typical of pious frauds.
You find many such frauds even in fundamental circles today. They
talk about the Lord leading them. My, sometimes the Lord "leads"
them to do some very unusual things! I find out sometimes that Christian men think they can do things that the Mafia would be arrested for.

But these men can very piously pray about it and *say* that it is the Lord's will. Believe me, Jacob at this point is a pious fraud. The Lord had nothing to do with this deception.

And Isaac said unto Jacob, Come near, I pray thee, that I may feel thee, my son, whether thou be my very son Esau or not.

And Jacob went near unto Isaac his father; and he felt him, and said, The voice is Jacob's voice, but the hands are the hands of Esau.

And he discerned him not, because his hands were hairy, as his brother Esau's hands: so he blessed him.

And he said, Art thou my very son Esau? And he said, I am.

And he said, Bring it near to me, and I will eat of my son's venison, that my soul may bless thee. And he brought it near to him, and he did eat: and he brought him wine, and he drank.

And his father Isaac said unto him, Come near now, and kiss me, my son.

And he came near, and kissed him: and he smelled the smell of his raiment, and blessed him, and said, See, the smell of my son is as the smell of a field which the LORD hath blessed [Gen. 27:21–27].

You can tell that Isaac suspected something was wrong, but Rebekah knew Isaac very well and she had worked out every detail.

Therefore God give thee of the dew of heaven, and the fatness of the earth, and plenty of corn and wine:

Let people serve thee, and nations bow down to thee: be lord over thy brethren, and let thy mother's sons bow

**down to thee: cursed be every one that curseth thee, and
blessed be he that blesseth thee [Gen. 27:28–29].**

Isaac is giving the blessing which *he* had received—he is passing it
on. The interesting thing is that it already belonged to Jacob. God had
said that it did. God had already blessed Jacob. God is not accepting
this deception at all.

**And it came to pass, as soon as Isaac had made an end
of blessing Jacob, and Jacob was yet scarce gone out
from the presence of Isaac his father, that Esau his
brother came in from his hunting.**

**And he also had made savoury meat, and brought it
unto his father, and said unto his father, Let my father
arise, and eat of his son's venison, that thy soul may
bless me.**

**And Isaac his father said unto him, Who art thou? And
he said, I am thy son, thy firstborn Esau.**

**And Isaac trembled very exceedingly, and said, Who?
where is he that hath taken venison, and brought it me,
and I have eaten of all before thou camest, and have
blessed him? yea, and he shall be blessed [Gen. 27:30–
33].**

Somebody may ask whether venison tastes like lamb or goat. It surely
does. I remember several years ago when I was pastor in Pasadena that
I went deer hunting in Utah with one of the officers of the church. We
got a deer, and so we invited the congregation for a dinner just to have
a time of good, wholesome fellowship and a lot of fun. We didn't have
quite enough meat for all the people; so we bought two lamb legs and
cooked that along with the rest of the meat. Nobody could tell the
difference, and everyone said the venison was good. Both meats
tasted very much alike.

Now Isaac really sees how he has been taken in by this plot.

And when Esau heard the words of his father, he cried with a great and exceeding bitter cry, and said unto his father, Bless me, even me also, O my father.

And he said, Thy brother came with subtilty, and hath taken away thy blessing.

And he said, Is not he rightly named Jacob? for he hath supplanted me these two times: he took away my birthright; and, behold, now he hath taken away my blessing. And he said, Hast thou not reserved a blessing for me?

And Isaac answered and said unto Esau, Behold, I have made him thy lord, and all his brethren have I given to him for servants; and with corn and wine have I sustained him: and what shall I do now unto thee, my son?

And Esau said unto his father, Hast thou but one blessing, my father? bless me, even me also, O my father. And Esau lifted up his voice, and wept.

And Isaac his father answered and said unto him, Behold, thy dwelling shall be the fatness of the earth, and of the dew of heaven from above;

And by thy sword shalt thou live, and shalt serve thy brother: and it shall come to pass when thou shalt have the dominion, that thou shalt break his yoke from off thy neck [Gen. 27:34–40].

JACOB FLEES TO LABAN

And Esau hated Jacob because of the blessing wherewith his father blessed him: and Esau said in his heart, The days of mourning for my father are at hand; then will I slay my brother Jacob [Gen. 27:41].

Esau is thinking: *My father is old and won't live much longer. Just as soon as my father dies, I'll kill Jacob. I'll get rid of him!* This is the thought of his heart, and he evidently talked about it to others.

And these words of Esau her elder son were told to Rebekah: and she sent and called Jacob her younger son, and said unto him, Behold, thy brother Esau, as touching thee, doth comfort himself, purposing to kill thee.

Now therefore, my son, obey my voice; and arise, flee thou to Laban my brother to Haran [Gen. 27:42–43].

Here again we see Rebekah taking things into her own hands. She tells Jacob, "You are going to have to leave home." Little did she know that she would pay for her part in this, her sin. She never saw this boy again. She said she would send him over there for a little while, but it was a long while and she died before he got back.

We must remember that Jacob is her favorite. She wants Jacob to go to her brother, Laban, and that is where she will send him. This is where Jacob is going to learn his lesson. This is where the chickens will come home to roost. Old Uncle Laban is going to put him through school and teach him a few things. Jacob thought he was clever, but Uncle Laban is an expert at cleverness. Poor Jacob will find he is just an amateur, and he is going to cry out to God in desperation before it is all over.

And tarry with him a few days, until thy brother's fury turn away:

Until thy brother's anger turn away from thee, and he forget that which thou hast done to him: then I will send, and fetch thee from thence: why should I be deprived also of you both in one day? [Gen. 27:44–45].

Notice that she says she will send him away for a few days. A few days lengthened to twenty years, and during that interval she died. She never saw her boy, her pet, her favorite, again.

We can picture the life of Rebekah during those years when we consider that Esau probably did not think much of his mother after that little episode.

And Rebekah said to Isaac, I am weary of my life because of the daughters of Heth: if Jacob take a wife of the daughters of Heth, such as these which are of the daughters of the land, what good shall my life do me? [Gen. 27:46].

Remember that Esau had married these heathen, godless women. Already that was bringing sorrow into the home, and even Rebekah was overwhelmed by it. Now she tells Isaac that if Jacob stays there he will probably do the same thing. She could use this as an excellent excuse to get Jacob away from home to protect him from Esau. She has this little conference with Isaac to convince him that the thing to do is to send Jacob back to her family, to her brother Laban. Remember how Abraham's servant had gone there to get her. So now the point is to get Jacob back there to find a wife, but also to get him out of danger. Very frankly, I think that if he had stayed at home, Esau would have tried to kill him. However, the way it turned out, Rebekah was the first to die, and Jacob got back for his father's funeral. But he never again saw his mother.

CHAPTER 28

THEME: God appears to Jacob at Bethel; Jacob makes a vow

In the previous chapter we saw Jacob doing one of the most despicable things any man could do. He did it at the behest of his mother. You know, sometimes people excuse themselves for being mean by saying it is because their mother didn't love them when they were little. Believe me, Jacob couldn't say that. Jacob was loved and spoiled. When he was asked to do something that was not the honorable thing to do, he did it. He stole the birthright from his brother.

The birthright was already his. The formality of his father giving a blessing wasn't necessary at all. Abraham hadn't given the blessing to Isaac—God had! And it is God who gave it to Jacob. His trickery was not only unnecessary, but God will deal with him because of it, you can be sure of that.

The plan that Rebekah has now thought of is plausible and logical. It probably was the right thing to do in this case. She didn't mention to Isaac that she wanted to send Jacob to her brother so that he'd get away from the wrath of his brother Esau, but she did mention the fact that he could choose a wife back there from among her family.

In this chapter we will find Jacob leaving home. He comes to Bethel where God appears to him and confirms to him the covenant made to Abraham.

And Isaac called Jacob, and blessed him, and charged him, and said unto him, Thou shalt not take a wife of the daughters of Canaan [Gen. 28:1].

All the way through the Old Testament we find that God does not want the godly to marry the ungodly. That, again, is my reason for believing that in the sixth chapter of Genesis, where it says the sons of God looked upon the daughters of men, it is saying that the godly line married with the godless line of Cain. This finally resulted in the judgment of the Flood with only one godly man left.

Intermarriage always leads to godlessness. I say this as a caution. I recognize that we are living in a day when young people are not very apt to take advice from an old preacher. They wonder what he knows about it all. Frankly, if you want to know the truth, I know a whole lot about this particular matter. I've done years of counseling and have had many, many couples come to me and have been able to watch them through the years. The story is pretty much the same. A young lady or a young man will say they have met the right person, the one they wish to marry. That person is not a Christian. However, they want to marry that person and win him or her for the Lord. May I say this, young lady, if you cannot win him for the Lord before you get married, you will not win him after you are married. May I say this, young man, if you cannot win her for the Lord before you get married, you will not win her after you are married. God forbids the godly to marry the godless. It always entails sorrow. I have seen literally hundreds of cases, and I have never yet seen a case where it has worked. Never yet! You can't beat God. God has put it down indelibly all the way through the Word that the godly are not to marry the godless. "Be ye not unequally yoked together with unbelievers: for what fellowship hath righteousness with unrighteousness? and what communion hath light with darkness?" (2 Cor. 6:14). The New Testament strictly tells Christians that they are not to be unequally yoked. You don't get unequally yoked by sitting on a platform with an unbeliever, as some critics have accused me of doing! You do it by intermarrying. That's the way you join up with them. And God strictly forbids it.

> **Arise, go to Padan-aram, to the house of Bethuel thy mother's father; and take thee a wife from thence of the daughters of Laban thy mother's brother.**

> **And God Almighty bless thee, and make thee fruitful, and multiply thee, that thou mayest be a multitude of people;**

> And give thee the blessing of Abraham, to thee, and to
> thy seed with thee; that thou mayest inherit the land
> wherein thou art a stranger, which God gave unto Abra-
> ham [Gen. 28:2–4].

It is obvious now that Isaac understands that God had given the blessing to Abraham, that God had transferred it to him, and that this blessing is to be passed on to his son, Jacob.

> And Isaac sent away Jacob: and he went to Padan-aram
> unto Laban, son of Bethuel the Syrian, the brother of
> Rebekah, Jacob's and Esau's mother [Gen. 28:5].

If you were to give the nationality of this family, you would have to say
they were Syrians because that is what they are called in the Scriptures. Sometimes the question is asked, "Was Abraham a Jew? Was he
an Israelite?" No, actually he was not. There were no Israelites until
the time of Jacob whose name was changed to Israel. His twelve sons
were Israelites. The line came from Abraham, he is the father of the
race, but you're not going to call Abraham a Midianite, I hope, and yet
he is the father of the Midianites, also.

> When Esau saw that Isaac had blessed Jacob, and sent
> him away to Padan-aram, to take him a wife from
> thence; and that as he blessed him he gave him a
> charge, saying; Thou shalt not take a wife of the daugh-
> ters of Canaan;
>
> And that Jacob obeyed his father and his mother, and
> was gone to Padan-aram;
>
> And Esau seeing that the daughters of Canaan pleased
> not Isaac his father;
>
> Then went Esau unto Ishmael, and took unto the wives
> which he had Mahalath the daughter of Ishmael Abra-
> ham's son, the sister of Nebajoth, to be his wife [Gen.
> 28:6–9].

Now lest someone misunderstand what I meant when I said we were through with the line of Ishmael, let me say that the Bible will not follow his line. However, his line will be mentioned as it crosses the line leading to Christ. So here, Esau goes out and marries the daughter of Ishmael. He thinks it will please his father. You see what a lack of spiritual perception he has. The Ishmaelites were as much rejected as the Canaanites or the Philistines.

GOD APPEARS TO JACOB AT BETHEL

And Jacob went out from Beer-sheba, and went toward Haran.

And he lighted upon a certain place, and tarried there all night, because the sun was set; and he took of the stones of that place, and put them for his pillows, and lay down in that place to sleep [Gen. 28:10–11].

The place he has come to, as we shall see in a moment, is Bethel, literally, "the House of God." Bethel is twelve miles north of Jerusalem, and the home which Jacob left was probably twenty-five or thirty miles south of Jerusalem. This means that Jacob covered at least forty miles that first day. You can see that he is really hotfooting it away from Esau. He wants to get as far from him as he can, but the farther he gets away from Esau, the farther he gets away from home.

What do you think he was feeling that night? Well, he was very lonely, that is for sure. He was probably homesick. As far as the record is concerned, this was his first night away from home.

My friend, do you remember the first night that you were away from home? I certainly remember the first night I went away from home. We lived in the country in a little place called Springer, Oklahoma. They tell me it hasn't done any springing since then. It's still a small place, just a wide place in the road. We had some very wonderful friends who lived down the road. I suppose it couldn't have been over a mile, but at that time I thought it was five or more miles. I've been back there, and I was amazed to find out how close together things are. When I was little, I thought it was all pretty well spread out. Well, these people invited me to come down and spend the night. They had a boy about my age—we were nine or ten, I guess. He had come up to get me, and we went down to his house together. I shall never forget that experience. We had a delicious dinner, a good country dinner, and I enjoyed it that evening with these folks. Then we played hide-and-seek until it got dark which kept me occupied, but every now and then I looked into the darkness and began to get just a little homesick. Then someone said it was time to go to bed. They put a pallet down in the front room, and I put on the little nightshirt that I had brought under my arm, and I lay down on that pallet. Friend, I have never been so lonely in all my life. Homesick! Oh, how I wanted to go home! I rolled and tossed there for a long time. I finally dozed off and I slept for a while, but I awoke very early in the morning. Do you know what I did? I took off my nightshirt and put on my clothes, put my nightshirt under my arm and started running home. I didn't stop until I got there. Nobody was up, but I was sure glad to be home. First night away from home. After that, I went a long way from home, but I never was more homesick than I was that first night.

I have often wondered about Jacob. He's actually a man now, a pretty big boy, but I think he is homesick. This is the first time he is away from Rebekah. He's been tied to his mama's apron strings all of his life, and now he is untied. He is out on his own, and this is his first night away from home.

Notice what happens. He lies down and puts stones for pillows. Bethel is a dreary place. It has been described as a bleak moorland with large, bare rocks exposed. It is twelve hundred feet above sea level, in the hills. There are many places out in the desert of California that would correspond to it.

When traveling around in the proximity of Bethel, I was with a bus tour. Others wanted to go other places which to me weren't nearly as important as Bethel. We drove within about a half mile of it and I wanted to walk to it, but the bus driver said we didn't have time. I could see it in the distance, and the topography looked bleak and forbidding. Yet this was the high point in the spiritual life of Jacob, not

only at this time but also later in his life. So this is the place he came
to, and here he lay down to sleep.

> **And he dreamed, and behold a ladder set up on the
> earth, and the top of it reached to heaven: and behold
> the angels of God ascending and descending on it.**

> **And, behold, the LORD stood above it, and said, I am the
> LORD God of Abraham thy father, and the God of Isaac:
> the land whereon thou liest, to thee will I give it, and to
> thy seed [Gen. 28:12-13].**

It was right in that area, by the way, where God first appeared to Abraham after he had reached the land of Palestine.

> **And thy seed shall be as the dust of the earth, and thou
> shalt spread abroad to the west, and to the east, and to
> the north, and to the south: and in thee and in thy seed
> shall all the families of the earth be blessed [Gen.
> 28:14].**

Now God is giving to Jacob exactly what He had given first to Abraham; He had repeated it to Isaac, and now He confirms it, and He
reaffirms to Jacob that He will do this

> **And, behold, I am with thee, and will keep thee in all
> places whither thou goest, and will bring thee again
> into this land; for I will not leave thee, until I have done
> that which I have spoken to thee of [Gen. 28:15].**

You can see that this would be comforting and helpful to a lonesome,
homesick boy who really had to leave home in a hurry. He is on his
way to a far country, and this first night God says to him, "I'm going to
be with you, Jacob, and I'm going to bring you back to this land."

The vision that God gave to him in the dream was of a ladder that reached up to heaven. What does that ladder mean? Well, the Lord Jesus interpreted it when He called Nathanael, as recorded in John 1:45–51. By the way, Nathanael was a wiseacre, and when he heard of Jesus, he said, "Can any good thing come out of Nazareth?" Our Lord dealt with this fellow. Nathanael asked, "How in the world do you know me like that?" And Jesus said, "Before Philip called you, when you were under the fig tree, I saw you." Nathanael's response was, "Rabbi, thou art the Son of God; thou art the King of Israel." He was pretty easy to convince, although he was a skeptic at the beginning. Let me give you the exact quote: "Jesus answered and said unto him, Because I said unto thee, I saw thee under the fig tree, believest thou? thou shalt see greater things than these. And he saith unto him, Verily, verily, I say unto you, Hereafter ye shall see heaven open, and the angels of God ascending and descending upon the Son of man" (John 1:50–51).

What is that ladder? That ladder is Christ. The angels were ascending and descending upon the Son of man. The angels ministered to Him; they were subject to His command. Nathanael will hear from the top of that ladder the voice of God, "This is my beloved Son in whom I am well pleased." My friend, God is speaking to mankind through Christ in our day. We cannot come to the Father directly. Every now and then I hear someone say in a testimony, "When I was converted, I came directly to God. I have access to God." We do not, my friend. We come through Christ; we have access to the Father through Christ. That is the only way we can get into God's presence. The Lord Jesus said, "... I am the way, the truth, and the life: no man cometh unto the Father, but by me" (John 14:6). The Lord Jesus Christ Himself is the ladder—not one that we can climb but one that we can trust.

This truth was given first to Jacob, the usurper. To Nathanael our Lord said, "You are an Israelite in whom there is no guile"—that is, no Jacob. Nathanael was a wiseacre, a humorist, but he was not a trickster like Jacob. But this man, Jacob—God is going to have to deal with him. God has given him this wonderful, glorious promise, but, oh, Jacob has so much to learn!

Isn't that true of all of us today? No wonder God has to school us. No wonder God has to discipline us. He scourges every son whom He receives. He disciplines. He did it to Abraham and He did it to Isaac. He is going to do it to Jacob. Up to this point, everything has been going Jacob's way. I received a letter from a couple who had lost their two-year-old boy suddenly one night. Up to that time everything had been going their way. They were church members, but they were hypocrites. So many people are just members of the church, yet they don't know the Lord personally. The Lord has to shake us. He allows trials to come to us to discipline us. They put iron in our backbone; they put courage in our lives and enable us to stand for God.

Jacob has a long way to go. Notice what he does—

And Jacob awaked out of his sleep, and he said, Surely the LORD is in this place; and I knew it not.

And he was afraid, and said, How dreadful is this place! this is none other but the house of God, and this is the gate of heaven [Gen. 28:16–17].

This is the passage of Scripture that I use many times in dedicating a new church. "How dreadful is this place!" I think I shock some people, especially when the congregation has come in to dedicate a lovely new facility. I get up and look around and say, "How dreadful is this place." During the rest of the time I try to win them back to being friends of mine by telling them that the place is dreadful only for a fellow like Jacob, a sinner, trying to run away from God. Every house of God, every church, ought to be a dreadful place to any sinner running away from God. It is the place where the sinner ought to be able to meet God, come face to face with God, through the Ladder who has been sent down from heaven, even Christ.

When Jacob ran away from home, he had a limited view of God. He thought that when he ran away from home, he was running away from God, also. But he found that he had not left God back home. He exclaimed, "Surely the LORD is in this place; and I knew it not!"

JACOB MAKES A VOW

And Jacob rose up early in the morning, and took the stone that he had put for his pillows, and set it up for a pillar, and poured oil upon the top of it.

And he called the name of that place Beth-el: but the name of that city was called Luz at the first [Gen. 28:18–19].

Now listen to Jacob. He has a lot to learn, and this is an evidence of it.

And Jacob vowed a vow, saying, If God will be with me, and will keep me in this way that I go, and will give me bread to eat, and raiment to put on,

So that I come again to my father's house in peace; then shall the LORD be my God [Gen. 28:20–21].

What is he doing? He wants to trade with God. He says, "Now, God, *if* You will do this for me. . . ." But God has already *told* him that He is going to do every one of these things for him—"I am going to keep you; I am going to bring you back to this land; I am going to give you this land; and I'm going to give you offspring." Then Jacob turns around and bargains with Him, "*If* You will do it, then I'll serve You."

God doesn't do business with us that way. He didn't do business that way with Jacob either. If He had, Jacob would never have made it back to that land. God brought him back into that land by His grace and mercy. When Jacob did finally come back to Bethel, he came back a wiser man. Do you know what he came back to do? To worship and praise God for His mercy. God had been merciful to him.

Many people even today say they will serve the Lord *if* He will do such and such. You won't do anything of the kind, my friend. He doesn't do business that way. He will extend mercy to you, and He will be gracious to you without asking anything in return. But He does say that if you love Him, you will really want to serve Him. That will be the bondage of love. It is the same kind of love a mother has for the little child. She becomes its slave. That's the way that He wants you and me.

And this stone, which I have set for a pillar, shall be God's house: and of all that thou shalt give me I will surely give the tenth unto thee [Gen. 28:22].

So Jacob erects this stone. He is trying to make a deal with God! And a great many of us are trying to make a deal with God. Oh, my friend, He just wants to become your *Father* through faith in Christ.

CHAPTER 29

THEME: Jacob meets Rachel; Jacob serves for Rachel; Jacob is deceived

Over this chapter I would like to write: "Be not deceived; God is not mocked: for whatsoever a man soweth, that shall he also reap. For he that soweth to his flesh shall of the flesh reap corruption; but he that soweth to the Spirit shall of the Spirit reap life everlasting" (Gal. 6:7–8). Probably the title that we ought to put over this chapter is "Chickens Come Home to Roost." In the beginning of this chapter we will see that Jacob begins to reap the harvest of his evil doing. The passage in Galatians is written primarily for Christians, but it expresses a universal law of God in every age. It is true in any area of life. You sow corn: you reap corn. You sow cotton; you reap cotton. You sow wheat; you reap wheat. You sow tares; you reap tares.

Examples of this principle run all the way through the Scriptures. For instance, Pharaoh slew the male children of the Hebrews, and in time his son was slain by the death angel. Ahab, through false accusations, had Naboth slain and the dogs licked his blood. God sent His prophet Elijah to Ahab with the message that, as the dogs had licked the blood of Naboth, they would lick the blood of Ahab. And that was literally fulfilled. You remember that David found this to be an inexorable law which was applicable to his own life. He committed the terrible sins of adultery and murder. God forgave him for his sin. Yet, the chickens came home to roost. He reaped what he had sown. His own daughter was raped and his son slain. Even Paul the apostle felt the weight of this law. He had given his consent at the stoning of Stephen. Later, Paul was taken outside the city of Lystra and was stoned and left for dead.

Jacob is the classic illustration of this inflexible law. Jacob had lived by his wits. He was rather cocky and clever. He had practiced deceit. He would stoop to use shady methods to accomplish his pur-

pose. And he was proud of his cleverness. But he will reap what he
has sown.

As we come to this chapter, Jacob leaves Bethel and resumes his
journey. After a period of time (I do not know how long), he arrives in
Haran.

> **Then Jacob went on his journey, and came into the land
> of the people of the east.**
>
> **And he looked, and behold a well in the field, and, lo,
> there were three flocks of sheep lying by it; for out of that
> well they watered the flocks: and a great stone was upon
> the well's mouth.**
>
> **And thither were all the flocks gathered: and they rolled
> the stone from the well's mouth, and watered the sheep,
> and put the stone again upon the well's mouth in his
> place [Gen. 29:1-3].**

We see here the importance of water in that country. It still is a very
important item because there is a shortage of it in many places. It must
be husbanded and protected; that is why at a certain time during the
day the stone was removed from the top of the well, and then everybody watered their sheep—everybody got the water he needed. Then
the stone was put back on to close the well.

Now Jacob arrives on the scene before they take the stone away
from the well. Believe me, he is as cocky as ever.

> **And Jacob said unto them, My brethren, whence be ye?
> And they said, Of Haran are we.**
>
> **And he said unto them, Know ye Laban the son of Na-
> hor? And they said, We know him [Gen. 29:4-5].**

Oh yes, they knew him. But Jacob didn't know him—yet. But, oh my,
Jacob is going to get acquainted with him.

> And he said unto them, Is he well? And they said, He is
> well: and, behold, Rachel his daughter cometh with the
> sheep.
>
> And he said, Lo, it is yet high day, neither is it time that
> the cattle should be gathered together: water ye the
> sheep, and go and feed them [Gen. 29:6–7].

Here Jacob has just arrived in the land and he is telling them how to
water their sheep and what they should do! This is typical of him, by
the way.

> And they said, We cannot, until all the flocks be gath-
> ered together, and till they roll the stone from the well's
> mouth; then we water the sheep [Gen. 29:8].

JACOB MEETS RACHEL

> And while he yet spake with them, Rachel came with
> her father's sheep: for she kept them [Gen. 29:9].

Rachel is a shepherdess who takes care of the sheep. This was woman's work in that day.

> And it came to pass, when Jacob saw Rachel the daugh-
> ter of Laban his mother's brother, and the sheep of La-
> ban his mother's brother, that Jacob went near, and
> rolled the stone from the well's mouth, and watered the
> flock of Laban his mother's brother [Gen. 29:10].

I don't know who told him to water the flock of Laban, but he did it.
Jacob is not following anyone's law but his own. He made the rules for
the game as he went through life—that is, the first part of his life. He
has a tremendous lesson to learn, and Uncle Laban is the one to teach
him.

And Jacob kissed Rachel, and lifted up his voice, and wept [Gen. 29:11].

This verse has always been strange to me. Frankly, kissing *that* girl and then weeping is hard for me to understand! However, I am of the opinion that this boy had had a lonely trip from the moment he had left home. We need to remember that from Bethel he had to go up by the Sea of Galilee, then up into Syria. He had to cross that desert. I suppose he had many experiences along the way. When he arrived, he was very cocky and greeted the men there in a matter-of-fact way as though he had known them all of their lives. He asks them questions, then probably in an officious way takes the stone from the mouth of the well. I suppose when he greeted this girl who was a member of his mother's family he welled up with emotion and wept. That is the only way I can explain it. But I am sure that the next time he kissed her he didn't weep!

And Jacob told Rachel that he was her father's brother, and that he was Rebekah's son: and she ran and told her father [Gen. 29:12].

You will notice that he calls himself her father's brother. The Hebrew does not make a lot of the distinctions we make today. We've got it reduced down to whether a person is a *kissing* cousin or not, but in that day if you were related, you were a brother. That is the way it is translated here and quite properly so. But in English we would say that Jacob was her father's nephew and that he was a son of Rebekah, her father's sister.

And it came to pass, when Laban heard the tidings of Jacob his sister's son, that he ran to meet him, and embraced him, and kissed him, and brought him to his house. And he told Laban all these things [Gen. 29:13].

I imagine that Jacob had quite a bit to talk about. I wouldn't be surprised to find that he entertained them at dinner with his story of how he tricked his brother to get his birthright, and how he used trickery to get the blessing, and how clever he was. Probably he told about that night at Bethel, too. "He told Laban all these things."

> **And Laban said to him, Surely thou art my bone and my flesh. And he abode with him the space of a month [Gen. 29:14].**

Laban was convinced now that this was his nephew, and he says, "You're my relative, so come in and make yourself at home."

Now a month goes by, and notice what happens. Jacob is not working. He's a nephew from a far country, and he's come over to visit his uncle. I suppose he felt that he ought to have free room and board there. During that time he's courting this girl, Rachel. At least, he certainly has been casting his eyes in that direction. And I think she was casting her eyes in his direction, too.

Now, I can imagine that it was one morning at breakfast when the next incident took place.

> **And Laban said unto Jacob, Because thou art my brother, shouldest thou therefore serve me for nought? tell me, what shall thy wages be? [Gen. 29:15].**

This Uncle Laban is clever. Who had said anything about going to work? Jacob hadn't. So Uncle Laban is very tactful and says that he doesn't want Jacob to work for him for nothing. He says that he will pay Jacob. Frankly, you don't live with Laban a month without making some sort of an arrangement to pay your board. Uncle Laban is a clever one also, and now he is going to deal with his nephew.

> **And Laban had two daughters: the name of the elder was Leah, and the name of the younger was Rachel [Gen. 29:16].**

Here we are introduced to another daughter, Leah. Uncle Laban has been watching this boy, and he has noted that his nephew has become very much interested in his daughter Rachel, the younger of the two. The next verse tells us why—

Leah was tender eyed; but Rachel was beautiful and well favoured [Gen. 29:17].

Rachel was a very beautiful girl. Leah was "tender eyed" which is a way of saying that she was not beautiful at all.

In college when we were reading Greek and studying some of the plays of Euripides, when a fellow wanted to say something very nice about his girl, we found in the play that he would call her "cow-eyed." I always laughed about that and thought that I would turn that over in my mind before I ever considered that a compliment. Well now, the next time you meet a cow, take a look at the eyes, and you will see they are beautiful. Ever since I read that play, I have never seen a cow with ugly eyes.

But Leah was not cow-eyed, she was "tender eyed" which meant that she was sort of an ugly duckling.

So Laban has these two daughters, and it is obvious that Jacob is in love with Rachel.

JACOB SERVES FOR RACHEL

And Jacob loved Rachel; and said, I will serve thee seven years for Rachel thy younger daughter [Gen. 29:18].

We find Jacob was quite moon-eyed. So that morning at breakfast, when Uncle Laban suggested he go to work, he had something in mind himself. He knew that the boy was in love with the girl; so I don't think he was at all surprised at Jacob's answer when he asked what his wages should be. Jacob was willing to work for seven years for Rachel. This man, Laban, was driving a hard bargain.

> And Laban said, It is better that I give her to thee, than
> that I should give her to another man: abide with me
> [Gen. 29:19].

Laban accepts that bargain.

Now this next verse tells us one of the loveliest things that is said about Jacob. Frankly, in the early years of Jacob's life, the only appearance of anything beautiful or fine or noble is his love for Rachel.

> And Jacob served seven years for Rachel; and they
> seemed unto him but a few days, for the love he had to
> her [Gen. 29:20].

You can just see this man working. I tell you, Uncle Laban had him working hard. He worked out in the cold, out in the rain and in all sorts of weather, but he always thought of that girl Rachel. There she was to meet him after a hard day. He was desperately in love with her.

> And Jacob said unto Laban, Give me my wife, for my
> days are fulfilled, that I may go in unto her.
>
> And Laban gathered together all the men of the place,
> and made a feast [Gen. 29:21–22].

JACOB IS DECEIVED

Now notice what Uncle Laban is doing—

> And it came to pass in the evening, that he took Leah his
> daughter, and brought her to him; and he went in unto
> her.
>
> And Laban gave unto his daughter Leah Zilpah his
> maid for an handmaid.

> And it came to pass, that in the morning, behold, it was Leah: and he said to Laban, What is this thou hast done unto me? did not I serve with thee for Rachel? wherefore then hast thou beguiled me?
>
> And Laban said, It must not be so done in our country, to give the younger before the firstborn [Gen. 29:23–26].

At the marriage ceremony in those days, the woman was veiled, heavily veiled, so that she couldn't be seen. Poor Jacob didn't see the girl he was getting until the next morning. Lo and behold, it wasn't Rachel—it was Leah! At the moment he saw he had been tricked. I wonder if he didn't recall something of his own father when he, Jacob, had pretended to be the elder. He deceived his father, and that was the reason he had to leave home. You see, God does not approve of that type of conduct. The chickens are now coming home to roost. Jacob pretended to be the elder when he was the younger. Now he thinks he's getting the younger and he gets the elder. The tables are turned now, and it has become an awful thing for Jacob. To Jacob it is a criminal act that Laban has done, but notice how Uncle Laban passes it off. He is an expert at this type of thing. He tells Jacob that there was a little matter in the contract, a clause in the fine print, that he had forgotten to mention to Jacob. It was a custom in their country that the elder daughter must marry first, and the younger daughter could not marry until the elder daughter was married. But Uncle Laban is willing to be very generous in his dealings; so he has an offer to make.

> Fulfil her week, and we will give thee this also for the service which thou shalt serve with me yet seven other years [Gen. 29:27].

This week, you see, is another seven years. Uncle Laban is getting his money's worth, isn't he? And poor Jacob is really going to school. But he is taking two wives which he shouldn't have done. He will be in trouble before it is over.

And Jacob did so, and fulfilled her week; and he gave him Rachel his daughter to wife also [Gen. 29:28].

Uncle Laban made Jacob serve twice as long as he originally agreed to. Seven years was long enough, but, believe me, *fourteen* years is a long time! This arrangement gave Jacob two wives.

You may be thinking, *Well, since this is in the Bible, God must approve of polygamy.* No, God does not approve of everything that is in the Bible—that may startle you. For instance, God didn't approve of the devil's lie. God didn't approve of David's sin, and He judged him for it. But the *record* of both events is inspired—literally, God-breathed. In other words, God said through the writer, Moses, exactly what He wanted to say. The thing that is inspired is the record of the words God gave to Moses to write down in this Book we call the Bible. In Genesis 29 God gave an accurate record: Jacob did have two wives, and it tells us the way it came about. That is where inspiration comes in. It does not mean that God approved of everything that is recorded in the Bible. Certainly God disapproved of Jacob's having more than one wife.

May I say to you, this man Jacob had plenty of trouble in his family from here on, and it all can be traced back to his own methods which he had used. The chickens are coming home to roost.

And when the Lord saw that Leah was hated, he opened her womb; but Rachel was barren.

And Leah conceived, and bare a son, and she called his name Reuben: for she said, Surely the Lord hath looked upon my affliction; now therefore my husband will love me [Gen. 29:31–32].

Leah is a sad person because she knows her husband loves Rachel rather than her. When she becomes the mother of Reuben, it brings joy to her heart, and she feels that Jacob will love her now.

Reuben is Jacob's firstborn, but he is not the one who will begin the line leading to Christ. Rather, it will be Leah's fourth son, Judah. Judah was the kingly line. David was in this line, and later on, the Lord Jesus Himself, according to the flesh, came from the line of Judah. Reuben lost his position as the firstborn because of his sin. Levi was the priestly tribe. Leah was the mother of some of the outstanding sons of Jacob.

CHAPTER 30

THEME: Birth of Jacob's sons; birth of Joseph to
Rachel; Jacob prepares to leave Laban

When we come to this chapter, we see that God is moving in spite
of Jacob's sin. God is not moving because of it, but in spite of it.
The theme of the chapter is the family of Jacob and the birth of his
sons. Jacob longs to leave Laban, and Jacob makes a shrewd bargain
with him.

BIRTH OF JACOB'S SONS

And when Rachel saw that she bare Jacob no children,
Rachel envied her sister; and said unto Jacob, Give me
children, or else I die [Gen. 30:1].

You see, a woman in that day was disgraced unless she had an offspring, and the more children she had, the better was her position.

And Jacob's anger was kindled against Rachel: and he
said, Am I in God's stead, who hath withheld from thee
the fruit of the womb?

And she said, Behold my maid Bilhah, go in unto her;
and she shall bear upon my knees, that I may also have
children by her [Gen. 30:2–3].

We find here Jacob and Rachel reverting to the practice of that day.
Remember that Abraham and Sarah had done the same thing. God did
not approve of it then, and He is not going to approve of it now. The
Bible gives us an accurate record, but that does not mean that God
approved of all that was done. In fact, it is quite obvious that He disapproved of this. My, the strife that we have already called to your atten-

tion in Abraham's family. It was also in the family of Isaac. Now it is in Jacob's family already—and he is in for a great deal more trouble.

The next verses of this chapter tell of the birth of two sons of Jacob by Bilhah, Rachel's handmaid; two sons by Zilpah, Leah's handmaid; and then the birth of two more sons by Leah.

> **And God remembered Rachel, and God hearkened to her, and opened her womb.**
>
> **And she conceived, and bare a son; and said, God hath taken away my reproach:**
>
> **And she called his name Joseph; and said, The Lord shall add to me another son [Gen. 30:22–24].**

This is the boy who will go down into the land of Egypt. We will follow him later in the book, as he is quite a remarkable person.

Later on Benjamin will be born to Rachel. We will conclude this chapter by listing the twelve sons of Jacob because they are important. The twelve tribes of Israel will come from them and finally the nation of Israel.

JACOB PREPARES TO LEAVE LABAN

> **And it came to pass, when Rachel had born Joseph, that Jacob said unto Laban, Send me away, that I may go unto mine own place, and to my country.**
>
> **Give me my wives and my children, for whom I have served thee, and let me go: for thou knowest my service which I have done thee [Gen. 30:25–26].**

Now listen to Uncle Laban—he's not through yet, you may be sure of that!

> **And Laban said unto him, I pray thee, if I have found favour in thine eyes, tarry: for I have learned by experi-**

ence that the LORD hath blessed me for thy sake [Gen.
30:27].

This is quite interesting. You may recall that Abimelech, king of
Gerar, found that he was blessed when Isaac was in his midst. Now
Uncle Laban has discovered that God is with Jacob and has blessed
him for Jacob's sake. So Uncle Laban says, "My boy, don't rush off;
don't leave me. I've been blessed, and I want to raise your wages."

**And he said, Appoint me thy wages, and I will give it
[Gen. 30:28].**

Jacob knows by now that, any time Uncle Laban makes a deal, he is
the one who will come off the winner. Jacob has learned this lesson,
and he wants to leave.

**And he said unto him, Thou knowest how I have served
thee, and how thy cattle was with me.**

**For it was little which thou hadst before I came, and it is
now increased unto a multitude; and the LORD hath
blessed thee since my coming: and now when shall I
provide for mine own house also? [Gen. 30:29–30].**

Listen to Jacob complaining. He is singing the blues! He is saying,
"All I've got out of all this service for you are two wives with their two
maids and a house full of boys." In fact, he has eleven boys at this
point. What in the world is he going to do? How is he going to feed
them? He says, "God has blessed you and He has prospered you, and I
don't have anything."

**And he said, What shall I give thee? And Jacob said,
Thou shalt not give me any thing: if thou wilt do this
thing for me, I will again feed and keep thy flock:**

**I will pass through all thy flock to-day, removing from
thence all the speckled and spotted cattle, and all the**

> brown cattle among the sheep, and the spotted and
> speckled among the goats: and of such shall be my hire
> [Gen. 30:31–32].

In other words, the pure breeds will be Laban's, but the offbreeds,
those that are not blue-ribbon cattle, will be Jacob's. Jacob said, "You
just let me have these, and that will be my wages." That sounds like a
pretty good proposition for Laban.

> So shall my righteousness answer for me in time to
> come, when it shall come for my hire before thy face:
> every one that is not speckled and spotted among the
> goats, and brown among the sheep, that shall be
> counted stolen with me.

> And Laban said, Behold, I would it might be according
> to thy word.

> And he removed that day the he goats that were ring-
> straked and spotted, and all the she goats that were
> speckled and spotted, and every one that had some
> white in it, and all the brown among the sheep, and gave
> them into the hand of his sons [Gen. 30:33–35].

They would not be able to breed with the others. Jacob would take the
off-breeds so that only the full breeds would mate and bear offspring,
and those would belong to Uncle Laban. The others would be his.
Jacob is making a very interesting deal.

> And he set three days' journey betwixt himself and
> Jacob: and Jacob fed the rest of Laban's flocks.

> And Jacob took him rods of green poplar, and of the
> hazel and chestnut tree; and pilled white strakes in
> them, and made the white appear which was in the
> rods.

> And he set the rods which he had pilled before the
> flocks in the gutters in the watering troughs when the

flocks came to drink, that they should conceive when they came to drink.

And the flocks conceived before the rods, and brought forth cattle ringstraked, speckled, and spotted [Gen. 30:36–39].

There have been various explanations of this. There are those who say this is nothing in the world but pure superstition. Others say it is an old wives' tale and is certainly something which ought not to be in the Bible record. It is my judgment that it is important that this record appears in the Word of God. Of course, there were genetic factors involved, but I don't feel that we should rule out this as being a superstition. The point is that both Laban and Jacob *believed* that the white streaks in the rods caused the offspring to be ringstraked. That is the important part of the story. Maybe you are too smart to believe it, but these two boys believed it. Regardless of whether or not there was value in it, Jacob is using trickery. He had been quite a trickster, but he has met an uncle who is a better trickster than he is, and now Jacob is trying to make a comeback.

This is all I will say about it at this point, and we will see that the next chapter will throw new light on this entire incident.

Now here is the list of Jacob's twelve sons who will eventually comprise the twelve tribes of the nation Israel.

Born to Leah: 1. Reuben
                 2. Simeon
                 3. Levi
                 4. Judah
                 5. Issachar
                 6. Zebulun
                 7. Dinah, daughter
Born to Bilhah, Rachel's maid:
                 1. Dan
                 2. Naphtali
Born to Zilpah, Leah's maid:
                 1. Gad
                 2. Asher

Born to Rachel: 1. Joseph
                        2. Benjamin

Believe me, Jacob had his hands full with these twelve boys! Also, we find that there was a girl, and her name was Dinah.

We will see in the next chapter that God has called Jacob to leave Haran and return to the land which He has promised to Abraham, to Isaac, and to Jacob. I am sure that God is thinking of Jacob's children—He doesn't want them to grow up in the environment of Laban's household.

CHAPTER 31

THEME: Jacob flees from Haran; the Mizpah covenant

In this chapter we find that Jacob leaves Laban without giving notice. They don't even have a farewell party for him. Laban takes out after him and overtakes him. Finally, Jacob and Laban made another contract, this time not to defraud or hurt each other. Then they separate in an outwardly friendly manner.

We will see that God wants to get Jacob out of that land. He recognizes that the influence of Laban's household is not good for Jacob and his growing family. The boys are going to be heads of the twelve tribes of Israel, and God is anxious to get them out from that environment and back into Abraham's country, the country which He had promised to Abraham.

We are in a section of the Word of God which God has given to minister to our needs. It deals with a man who is a very sinful man in many ways and a man whom God would not give up. You and I can take courage from this. The Lord will never give us up as long as we keep coming back to Him. He will always receive us. If He will take a fellow like Jacob and a fellow like I am, He will take you, my friend.

You will recall that Jacob has had a pretty sad ordeal of twenty years with Uncle Laban. Uncle Laban has really given him a course in the college of hard knocks, and poor Jacob is beginning to wince because of all the pressure he has been under. However, since the new deal which he had made with Laban regarding cattle breeding, Jacob is now getting more than Uncle Laban is getting. Uncle Laban doesn't like it, nor do his sons like it.

And he heard the words of Laban's sons, saying, Jacob hath taken away all that was our father's; and of that which was our father's hath he gotten all this glory.

> And Jacob beheld the countenance of Laban, and, behold, it was not toward him as before [Gen. 31:1–2].

Now Jacob has a call from God.

> And the LORD said unto Jacob, Return unto the land of thy fathers, and to thy kindred; and I will be with thee.

> And Jacob sent and called Rachel and Leah to the field unto his flock [Gen. 31:3–4].

God called Jacob to leave, and so he is now preparing to do that. He calls Rachel and Leah to meet him in the field because he is afraid to talk this over at home for fear some servant or possibly even Laban or Laban's sons might overhear him. He doesn't want them to see him plotting with Rachel and Leah.

> And said unto them, I see your father's countenance, that it is not toward me as before; but the God of my father hath been with me.

> And ye know that with all my power I have served your father [Gen. 31:5–6].

That is one thing upon which we can agree with Jacob and say to his credit. He had worked hard, but I'm of the opinion that we ought to give Laban credit for that. I believe that Laban got his money's worth out of anyone who worked for him.

> And your father hath deceived me, and changed my wages ten times; but God suffered him not to hurt me [Gen. 31:7].

Notice that ten times in those twenty years old Laban had changed his wages! Poor Jacob. But when he was perplexed and frustrated, not knowing where to turn, God intervened.

If he said thus, The speckled shall be thy wages; then all the cattle bare speckled: and if he said thus, The ring-straked shall be thy hire; then bare all the cattle ring-straked.

Thus God hath taken away the cattle of your father, and given them to me [Gen. 31:8-9].

Jacob is explaining to Rachel and Leah that it is God who has blessed him, to the extent that Laban and his sons have become very jealous of him; in fact, they hate him.

Now Jacob tells the actual reason why he wants to leave—

And the angel of God spake unto me in a dream, saying, Jacob: And I said, Here am I.

And he said, Lift up now thine eyes, and see, all the rams which leap upon the cattle are ringstraked, speckled, and grisled: for I have seen all that Laban doeth unto thee [Gen. 31:11-12].

You probably thought that in the previous chapter I was not giving a satisfactory answer for what had taken place in the breeding of cattle. I was waiting until we came to this portion of Scripture, because God says, "I did it!" We don't need to look for natural explanations, although I am confident that God used one of them. However, since God didn't tell us which one it is, we simply do not know. There are several explanations, and you may take the one you want, but I like this one: God says, "I saw what Laban was doing to you, and I blessed you."

I am the God of Beth-el, where thou anointedst the pillar, and where thou vowedst a vow unto me: now arise, get thee out from this land, and return unto the land of thy kindred [Gen. 31:13].

"I am the God of Beth-el." God goes back to the time He appeared to this boy when he was running away, that first night away from home which he spent at Bethel.

"Now arise, get thee out from this land, and return unto the land of thy kindred." God wants him to leave Haran because he has at this time eleven boys who are growing up, and they are already beginning to learn some things which they should not be learning. God wants to get Jacob and these boys away from the place of idolatry just as He got Abraham out of a home of idolatry.

> **And Rachel and Leah answered and said unto him, Is there yet any portion or inheritance for us in our father's house?**

> **Are we not counted of him strangers? for he hath sold us, and hath quite devoured also our money [Gen. 31:14–15].**

They are saying that certainly, as the daughters of their father, they should receive some inheritance, and that ought to keep Laban from being so antagonistic. But, friend, old Laban cannot be trusted.

Unfortunately, there are many Christians today who demonstrate in the way they handle their own money and the money of others that they cannot be trusted either. This is, I feel, a real test of an individual. I could tell you some stories that would make your hair stand on end. Christians, and Christian leaders, do things with money that ought not to be done.

> **For all the riches which God hath taken from our father, that is ours, and our children's: now then, whatsoever God hath said unto thee, do [Gen. 31:16].**

I admire these two women. They tell Jacob to do whatever he wants to do. They stand with him, and apparently they feel that their father has robbed them.

JACOB FLEES FROM HARAN

Then Jacob rose up, and set his sons and his wives upon camels;

And he carried away all his cattle, and all his goods which he had gotten, the cattle of his getting, which he had gotten in Padan-aram, for to go to Isaac his father in the land of Canaan.

And Laban went to shear his sheep: and Rachel had stolen the images that were her father's [Gen. 31:17–19].

Here is a revelation of something that is quite interesting. Jacob rises up and leaves posthaste again. You remember that this is the same way he left home when he was escaping from his brother. Now he is leaving his uncle—but it is not all his fault this time. It is obvious that he is prepared for this. He has all the cattle and the servants ready to march.

"Rachel had stolen the images that were her father's." I told you that they were in a home of idolatry. God didn't want Jacob's boys to be brought up there. But, you see, Rachel had been brought up in a home of idolatry, and she wanted to take her gods with her. What a primitive notion she had! Even Jacob had thought that he could run away from God when he left his home as a boy. But at Bethel God appeared to him. He found that he couldn't run away from God. In fact many years later David wrote: "Whither shall I go from thy spirit? or whither shall I flee from thy presence? If I ascend up into heaven, thou art there: if I make my bed in hell [sheol], behold, thou art there" (Ps. 139:7–8). That is, death won't separate you. "If I take the wings of the morning, and dwell in the uttermost parts of the sea; Even there shall thy hand lead me, and thy right hand shall hold me" (Ps. 139:9–10). You won't get away from God by even going to the moon. You simply cannot get away from Him.

"And Laban went to shear his sheep." Jacob waited until Laban went out to shear sheep. Probably Laban went quite a few miles away from home because the sheep grazed over a very large area in that day. They still do, for that matter, because it takes a large area to feed them. While Laban is away from home, Jacob just "forgets" to tell him that he is leaving.

And Jacob stole away unawares to Laban the Syrian, in that he told him not that he fled.

So he fled with all that he had; and he rose up, and passed over the river, and set his face toward the mount Gilead [Gen. 31:20–21].

They have come within sight of Mt. Gilead, which is just east of the Jordan River. They have covered a lot of ground.

And it was told Laban on the third day that Jacob was fled.

And he took his brethren with him, and pursued after him seven days' journey; and they overtook him in the mount Gilead [Gen. 31:22–23].

Laban really had been traveling fast to overtake him. You may be sure that Laban doesn't mean any good as far as Jacob is concerned. I am of the opinion that he is angry enough to kill him. But God intervened—

And God came to Laban the Syrian in a dream by night, and said unto him, Take heed that thou speak not to Jacob either good or bad [Gen. 31:24].

In other words, "You be very careful what you say and do."

Then Laban overtook Jacob. Now Jacob had pitched his tent in the mount: and Laban with his brethren pitched in the mount of Gilead [Gen. 21:25].

Listen to Uncle Laban. He's a clever rascal, by the way. He's been coming, breathing out fire and brimstone, and wanting to recover all the possessions which Jacob had taken. He probably wanted to kill Jacob and take back the two daughters and their children.

And Laban said to Jacob, What hast thou done, that thou hast stolen away unawares to me, and carried away my daughters, as captives taken with the sword?

Wherefore didst thou flee away secretly, and steal away from me; and didst not tell me, that I might have sent thee away with mirth, and with songs, with tabret, and with harp? [Gen. 31:26–27]

How clever Uncle Laban is, how diplomatic! He tries to make Jacob feel guilty for depriving his family of a wonderful send-off party. He would have had a great celebration and a fond farewell. That's what he *says*, but I don't think that is what he would have done. Then he goes on to appeal to sentiment.

And hast not suffered me to kiss my sons and my daughters? thou hast now done foolishly in so doing [Gen. 31:28].

These "sons" would be his grandsons. They are destined to be very prominent as far as the history of this world is concerned.

It is in the power of my hand to do you hurt: but the God of your father spake unto me yesternight, saying, Take thou heed that thou speak not to Jacob either good or bad [Gen. 31:29].

Laban lets him know that he didn't mean good by him but that God had prevented him from doing bad.

And now, though thou wouldest needs be gone, because thou sore longedst after thy father's house, yet wherefore hast thou stolen my gods? [Gen. 31:30].

Now he asks about the stolen gods. Actually, Jacob didn't know that Rachel had stolen the gods. When he answers Laban, he is answering about his running away without letting him know.

And Jacob answered and said to Laban, Because I was afraid: for I said, Peradventure thou wouldest take by force thy daughters from me [Gen. 31:31].

Jacob knew that Laban wouldn't have let him take his wives and his family and that which belonged to him.

Now he replies to the charge of the stolen gods—

With whomsoever thou findest thy gods, let him not live: before our brethren discern thou what is thine with me, and take it to thee. For Jacob knew not that Rachel had stolen them [Gen. 31:32].

He is sure no one would have stolen them from Laban. You see, Jacob didn't believe Laban. But if you think that Laban believed Jacob, you're wrong. They had absolutely no confidence in each other. It's been a nice, pleasant twenty years together, hasn't it?

And Laban went into Jacob's tent, and into Leah's tent, and into the two maidservants' tents; but he found them not. Then went he out of Leah's tent, and entered into Rachel's tent.

Now Rachel had taken the images, and put them in the camel's furniture, and sat upon them. And Laban searched all the tent, but found them not.

And she said to her father, Let it not displease my lord that I cannot rise up before thee; for the custom of

women is upon me. And he searched, but found not the
images [Gen. 31:33–35].

He really expected one of his daughters to have them. Rachel is quite a
clever girl herself, isn't she? She is the daughter of her father! She had
taken them and put them in the camel's furniture, which is the box
that went on the camel's back. Then she sat down on them and ex-
cused herself to her father. She said she couldn't get up because she
didn't feel well that day. All the while, she is sitting on them. What a
realistic picture we get of this family!

Rachel's taking the teraphim from her father was probably much
more serious than we had imagined. The possession of those household gods implied leadership of the family, which meant that Jacob
was going to inherit everything old Laban had! That is the reason Laban was so wrought up over it. He surely did not want Jacob to get his
estate—he felt he had gotten too much already.

Jacob gets a little confidence now. They can't locate the images,
and Jacob is sure that they aren't anywhere around. He wants to re-
buke his father-in-law who has come after him.

> And Jacob was wroth, and chode with Laban: and Jacob
> answered and said to Laban, What is my trespass? what
> is my sin, that thou hast so hotly pursued after me?
> [Gen. 31:36].

Now Jacob voices his complaint. He has passed the course in the college of hard knocks, and now he is getting his degree.

> This twenty years have I been with thee; thy ewes and
> thy she goats have not cast their young, and the rams
> of thy flock have I not eaten [Gen. 31:38].

He didn't even get his meals. He had to pay for those.

> That which was torn of beasts I brought not unto thee; I
> bare the loss of it; of my hand didst thou require it,
> whether stolen by day, or stolen by night [Gen. 31:39].

He couldn't even get any insurance. When a lamb was stolen or killed by a wild animal, Jacob had to pay for it. Believe me, this Laban is a hard taskmaster!

Thus I was; in the day the drought consumed me, and the frost by night; and my sleep departed from mine eyes [Gen. 31:40].

He didn't get a vacation in the summer. When the weather grew cold, he still had to stay out with the sheep and with the animals. Many nights he had to watch to protect the flock.

Thus have I been twenty years in thy house; I served thee fourteen years for thy two daughters, and six years for thy cattle: and thou hast changed my wages ten times [Gen. 31:41].

This is what has happened to Jacob. Here is the man who is clever, who thought that he could get by with sin, but God didn't let him get by with it because God has made it very clear that whatsoever a man sows, that shall he also reap. Jacob refused submission to God at home; so he had to submit to his uncle. Jacob came to receive a wife in dignity, but he was made a servant because God respects the rights of the firstborn. Jacob had deceived his father; so he was deceived by his father-in-law. Jacob, the younger, became as the older. Then he found out that he was given the older when he thought he was getting the younger. He revealed a mercenary spirit that displayed itself in the way he got the birthright, allowing his mother to cover his hands with the skins of kids of goats. Later on, we will see that his own sons will deceive him in very much the same way. They killed a kid and in its blood they dipped Joseph's coat of many colors. He deceived his father about being the favorite son, and he will be deceived about his favorite son, Joseph. Whatsoever a man sows, that shall he also reap.

Except the God of my father, the God of Abraham, and the fear of Isaac, had been with me, surely thou hadst

sent me away now empty. God hath seen mine affliction and the labour of my hands, and rebuked thee yesternight [Gen. 31:42].

Jacob has had his day in court. He has vented his grievances. Now he is going to leave Laban. They bid each other good-bye and make a contract.

THE MIZPAH COVENANT

And Laban answered and said unto Jacob, These daughters are my daughters, and these children are my children, and these cattle are my cattle, and all that thou seest is mine: and what can I do this day unto these my daughters, or unto their children which they have born?

Now therefore come thou, let us make a covenant, I and thou; and let it be for a witness between me and thee [Gen. 31:43–44].

Jacob set up a stone for a pillar, a heap of stones was gathered, and a contract was made.

And Laban said, This heap is a witness between me and thee this day. Therefore was the name of it called Galeed;

And Mizpah; for he said, The LORD watch between me and thee, when we are absent one from another [Gen. 31:48–49].

The words of this contract have been used by young people's groups and other groups as a benediction. I don't think it ought to be used that way because it was a contract made between two rascals who are going to quit stealing from each other and work on somebody else!

"The Lord watch between me and thee" is really saying, "May the Lord keep His eye on you so you won't steal from me anymore." That is exactly what these men are saying. And after this, they separate. The pile of stones remained at Mizpah as a boundary line between Laban and Jacob. Each promised not to cross over on the other's side.

CHAPTER 32

THEME: Crisis in the life of Jacob; wrestling at Peniel; Jacob's name changed to Israel

Chapter 32 is the high point in the life of Jacob and can be called the turning point in his life. However, this is not Jacob's conversion, by any means. In spite of the fact that he was living in the flesh, this man was still God's man. This is the reason that we are told to be very careful about judging folk as to whether they are Christians or not. There are a lot of people who do not look like they are Christians, but I am almost sure that they are. Whether they are or not is in the hands of the Lord. They just don't act like Christians—that's all; they give no evidence that they are. And this man Jacob gave no such evidence, except in very faint instances when God appeared to him and he did respond in a way.

Jacob, who is God's representative and witness in the world, has been a bad witness, but he cannot continue that way, and so God is going to deal with him. To tell the truth, God will cripple him in order to get him. The Lord also disciplines us: "For whom the Lord loveth he chasteneth . . ." (Heb. 12:6). That is His method. He disciplines in that way. Lot also did not look like he was a child of God—but he was, for Peter says that Lot "vexed his righteous soul" (see 2 Pet. 2:7–8). But I tell you, Lot certainly was put through the fire. He escaped the fire of Sodom and Gomorrah, but the Lord put him through the fires of testing. This is Jacob's experience also. He got his college degree at the college of hard knocks. Uncle Laban was president and dean of the school. At graduation, this boy Jacob gave a pitiful valedictorian address. It took him twenty years to get his degree, and he certainly worked for it. Old Laban changed the requirements ten times. Every two years, Jacob had a new contract with Uncle Laban, and it was always to Jacob's disadvantage. This was the experience of this man.

We come now to this test in which God is going to have to deal with Jacob because he is going to represent God. God will deal with him and will move in on him in this thirty-second chapter. At the beginning, I would like to write this verse of Scripture over this chapter: "He giveth power to the faint; and to them that have no might he increaseth strength" (Isa. 40:29). This is the experience of Jacob.

CRISIS IN THE LIFE OF JACOB

And Jacob went on his way, and the angels of God met him.

And when Jacob saw them, he said, This is God's host: and he called the name of that place Mahanaim [Gen. 32:1–2].

God is beginning to deal with Jacob directly in order to bring him into the place of fruit bearing and of real, vital service and witness for Him.

And Jacob sent messengers before him to Esau his brother unto the land of Seir, the country of Edom.

And he commanded them, saying, Thus shall ye speak unto my lord Esau; Thy servant Jacob saith thus, I have sojourned with Laban, and stayed there until now:

And I have oxen, and asses, flocks, and menservants, and womenservants: and I have sent to tell my lord, that I may find grace in thy sight [Gen. 32:3–5].

This fellow Jacob is still clever, isn't he? He just cannot let go, even after his experience with Laban. He is returning back to the land, and he remembers the last time he saw Esau twenty years ago, when Esau was breathing out threatenings against him. Notice that Jacob sends servants and instructs them, saying, "When you get to Esau my brother, say to him, 'My lord Esau.'" Of all things! And then he has them refer to himself as "Thy servant Jacob." That's not the way Jacob had spoken before. He had manipulated for the birthright and had stolen the blessing. He had been a rascal, but *now* his talk is different. I guess he had learned a few things from Uncle Laban. "My lord Esau . . . thy servant Jacob."

> **And the messengers returned to Jacob, saying, We came to thy brother Esau, and also he cometh to meet thee, and four hundred men with him [Gen. 32:6].**

This message absolutely frightened poor Jacob because he didn't know what all that meant. Esau did not indicate his intentions to the servants at all. I suppose that Jacob quizzed them rather thoroughly and said, "Did you detect any note of animosity or bitterness or hatred toward me?" And I suppose that one of the servants said, "No, he seemed to be glad to get the information that you were coming to meet him, and now he's coming to meet you." But the fact that Esau appeared glad was no comfort to Jacob. It could mean that Esau would be glad for the opportunity of getting revenge. Anyway, poor Jacob is upset.

> **Then Jacob was greatly afraid and distressed: and he divided the people that was with him, and the flocks, and herds, and the camels, into two bands;**
>
> **And said, If Esau come to the one company, and smite it, then the other company which is left shall escape [Gen. 32:7–8].**

Jacob is in a bad way, he thinks. With this brother of his coming to him, he divides up his group. He is being clever. He reasons that if his brother strikes one group, then the other one can escape.

Notice what Jacob does now. He appeals to God in his distress:

> **And Jacob said, O God of my father Abraham, and God of my father Isaac, the LORD which saidst unto me, Return unto thy country, and to thy kindred, and I will deal well with thee:**

**I am not worthy of the least of all the mercies, and of all
the truth, which thou hast shewed unto thy servant; for
with my staff I passed over this Jordan; and now I am
become two bands [Gen. 32:9–10].**

This man now appeals to God and cries out to Him on the basis that
He is the God of his father Abraham and the God of his father Isaac. I
begin now to detect a little change in Jacob's life. This is the first time
I have ever heard him say, "I am not worthy of the least of thy mercies."
For the first time, he is acknowledging that he might be a sinner in
God's sight. Do you know that there are a great many "Christians"
who do not acknowledge that they are sinners? For years I knew a man
who was incensed that I would indicate that he was a sinner. He told
me all that he had done and that he had been saved and now was not a
sinner. My friend, he is a sinner. We are all sinners, *saved by grace*. As
long as we are in this life, we have that old nature that isn't even fit
to go to heaven. And do you know that God is not going to let it go to
heaven? Vernon McGee cannot go there. That is the reason God had to
give me a new nature; the old one wasn't even fit to repair. This fellow
Jacob is beginning now to say that he is not worthy. When any man
begins to move toward God on that basis, he will find that God will
communicate with him.

Jacob makes this very interesting statement: "for with my staff I
passed over this Jordan; and now I am become two bands." He went
over the Jordan with just his walking stick, his staff—that's all he had.
Now he is coming back, and he has become two companies. This is
Jacob for you.

**Deliver me, I pray thee, from the hand of my brother,
from the hand of Esau: for I fear him, lest he will come
and smite me, and the mother with the children.**

**And thou saidst, I will surely do thee good, and make
thy seed as the sand of the sea, which cannot be num-
bered for multitude [Gen. 32:11–12].**

Jacob really cried out to God. That night was a very difficult night for him, and he didn't have any aspirins he could take.

And he lodged there that same night; and took of that which came to his hand a present for Esau his brother;

Two hundred she goats, and twenty he goats, two hundred ewes, and twenty rams,

Thirty milch camels with their colts, forty kine, and ten bulls, twenty she asses, and ten foals [Gen. 32:13–15].

Jacob is pretty generous with his stock now.

And he delivered them into the hand of his servants, every drove by themselves; and said unto his servants, Pass over before me, and put a space betwixt drove and drove [Gen. 32:16].

This is Jacob's tactic. He will send out a drove, a very rich gift, for his brother, and when that first drove arrives, Esau will say, "What is this?" The servants will reply, "We are bringing you a gift from your brother Jacob." Esau will receive that gift and then ride on a little farther to meet another drove of the same size. He will ask the servants, "Where are you going?" They will say, "We're going to meet Esau with a gift from his brother Jacob." And he will say, "I am Esau." Believe me, by the time Esau gets down where Jacob and the family are, he will be softened.

Jacob has prayed to God and has reminded the Lord, "You told me to return to my country. You said You would protect me." But does he believe God? No. He goes right ahead and makes these arrangements, which reveals that he isn't trusting God at all. I am afraid that we are often in the same position. Many of us take our burdens to the Lord in prayer. We just spread them out before Him—I do that. Then when we get through praying, we get right up and put each little burden right back on our back and start out again with them. We don't really believe Him, do we? We don't really trust Him as we should.

And he commanded the foremost, saying, When Esau my brother meeteth thee, and asketh thee, saying, Whose art thou? and whither goest thou? and whose are these before thee?

Then thou shalt say, They be thy servant Jacob's; it is a present sent unto my lord Esau: and, behold, also he is behind us.

And so commanded he the second, and the third, and all that followed the droves, saying, On this manner shall ye speak unto Esau, when ye find him.

And say ye moreover, Behold, thy servant Jacob is behind us. For he said, I will appease him with the present that goeth before me, and afterward I will see his face; peradventure he will accept of me [Gen. 32:17–20].

Esau will be met by one drove after another like that. This is the plan that Jacob is working on.

So went the present over before him: and himself lodged that night in the company.

And he rose up that night, and took his two wives, and his two womenservants, and his eleven sons, and passed over the ford Jabbok.

And he took them, and sent them over the brook, and sent over that he had [Gen. 32:21–23].

This is the night of the great experience in Jacob's life. The land where he crossed the Brook Jabbok is very desolate. When I was there, I purposely got away from my group and took a walk across the bridge that is there today. The United States built a very lovely road through that area for the Hashimite Kingdom of Jordan. There are several things in that area which you would not be able to see if there wasn't that good road, because it is quite a wilderness area. I took pictures of sheep that were drinking down at the Brook Jabbok. The crossing there is a very bleak place, right down between two hills, in that very mountainous and very rugged country. Here is where Jacob came that night. He is not a happy man, and he is filled with fear and doubts. You see, chickens are coming home to roost. He had mistreated Esau. God had never told him to get the birthright or the blessing in the way he did it. God would have gotten it for him. That night Jacob sends all that he has across the Brook Jabbok, but he stays on the other side so that, if his brother Esau comes, he might kill Jacob but spare the family. And so Jacob is left alone.

WRESTLING AT PENIEL

And Jacob was left alone; and there wrestled a man with him until the breaking of the day [Gen. 32:24].

There are several things I would like to get straight as we come to this wrestling match. I have heard it said that Jacob did the wrestling. Actually, Jacob didn't want to wrestle anybody. He has Uncle Laban in back of him who doesn't mean good at all, and he has his brother Esau ahead of him. Jacob is no match for either one. He is caught now between a rock and a hard place, and he doesn't know which way to turn. Do you think he wanted to take on a third opponent that night? I don't think so.

Years ago *Time* magazine, reporting in the sports section concerning the votes for the greatest wrestler, said that not a vote went to the most famous athlete in history, wrestling Jacob. Lo and behold, the magazine received a letter from someone who wrote asking them to tell something about this wrestler Jacob. The writer of the letter had never heard of him before! And evidently he had never read his Bible at all. Jacob is no wrestler—let's make that very clear here at the beginning. That night he was alone because he wanted to be alone, and he wasn't looking for a fight.

This is the question: Who is this one who wrestled with Jacob that night? There has been a great deal of speculation about who it is, but I think He is none other than the preincarnate Christ. There is some evidence for this in the prophecy of Hosea: "Ephraim feedeth on wind, and followeth after the east wind: he daily increaseth lies and desolation; and they do make a covenant with the Assyrians, and oil is carried into Egypt. The LORD hath also a controversy with Judah, and will punish Jacob according to his ways; according to his doings will he recompense him. He took his brother by the heel in the womb, and by his strength he had power with God: Yea, he had power over the angel, and prevailed: he wept, and made supplication unto him: he found him in Beth-el, and there he spake with us; Even the LORD God of hosts; the LORD is his memorial" (Hos. 12:1–5). "The LORD is his memorial"—or, "the Lord is His name." It was none other than Jehovah, the preincarnate Christ, who wrestled with Jacob that night.

> **And when he saw that he prevailed not against him, he touched the hollow of his thigh; and the hollow of Jacob's thigh was out of joint, as he wrestled with him [Gen. 32:25].**

Old Jacob is not going to give up easily; he is not that kind of man— and he struggled against Him. Finally, this One who wrestled with him crippled him.

> **And he said, Let me go, for the day breaketh. And he said, I will not let thee go, except thou bless me [Gen. 32:26].**

What happens now? Jacob is just holding on; he's not wrestling. He is just holding on to this One. He found out that you do not get anywhere with God by struggling and resisting. The only way that you get anywhere with Him is by yielding and just holding on to Him. Abraham had learned that, and that is why he said amen to God. He believed God, and He counted it to him for righteousness. Abraham reached the end of his rope and put his arms around God. My friend, when you get in that condition, then you trust God. When you are willing to hold on, He is there ready to help you.

JACOB'S NAME CHANGED TO ISRAEL

And he said unto him, What is thy name? And he said, Jacob.

And he said, Thy name shall be called no more Jacob, but Israel: for as a prince hast thou power with God and with men, and hast prevailed [Gen. 32:27–28].

·He is not Jacob anymore—the one who is usurper, the trickster—but Israel, "for as a prince hast thou power with God and with men, and hast prevailed." Now the new nature of Israel will be manifested in the life of this man.

And Jacob asked him, and said, Tell me, I pray thee, thy name. And he said, Wherefore is it that thou dost ask after my name? And he blessed him there.

And Jacob called the name of the place Peniel: for I have seen God face to face, and my life is preserved [Gen. 32:29–30].

Jacob had seen the Angel of the Lord, the preincarnate Christ.

And as he passed over Penuel the sun rose upon him, and he halted upon his thigh.

Therefore the children of Israel eat not of the sinew which shrank, which is upon the hollow of the thigh, unto this day: because he touched the hollow of Jacob's thigh in the sinew that shrank [Gen. 32:31–32].

God had to cripple Jacob in order to get him, but He got him. This man Jacob refused to give in at first—that was typical of him. He knew a few holds, and he thought that after awhile he would be able to overcome. Finally, he found out he couldn't overcome, but he would not surrender. And so what did God do? Certainly, with His superior strength, in a moment God could have pinned down Jacob's shoulders—but He wouldn't have pinned down his *will*. Jacob was like the little boy whose mama made him sit in a corner in his room. After awhile she heard a noise in there, and she called to him, "Willie, are you sitting down?" He said, "Yes, I'm sitting down, but I'm standing up on the inside of me!" That is precisely what would have happened to Jacob. He would have been standing up on the inside of himself—he wasn't ready to yield.

Notice how God deals with him. He touches the hollow of Jacob's thigh. Just a touch of the finger of God, and this man becomes helpless. But you see, God is not pinning down his shoulders. Now Jacob holds on to Him. The Man says, "Let Me go," and Jacob says, "No, I want Your blessing." He's clinging to God now. The struggling and striving are over, and from here on Jacob is going to manifest a spiritual nature, dependence upon God. You will not find the change happening in a moment's notice. Psychologists tell us that certain synaptic connections are set up in our nervous systems so that we do things by habit. We are creatures of habit. This man will lapse back into his old ways many times, but we begin to see something different in him now. Before we are through with him, we will find that he is a real man of God.

First, we saw him at his home and then in the land of Haran where he was a man of the flesh. Here at Peniel, at the Brook Jabbok, we find him fighting. After this, and all the way through down into Egypt, we see him as a man of faith. First a man of the flesh, then a man who is fighting and struggling, and finally a man of faith.

In the New Testament another young man, a son of Jacob by the name of Saul of Tarsus, tells us his struggle in chapter 7 of Romans. There were three periods in his life. When he was converted, he thought he could live the Christian life. That's where I made my mistake also. When I became a Christian, I frankly thought I could live the Christian life. After all, Vernon McGee didn't need any help. I thought it was easy, but I didn't *do* it, and that was the hard part. That is where Paul had his problem: "For the good that I would I do not: but the evil which I would not, that I do" (Rom. 7:19).

Paul found out that not only was there no good in the old nature, but there also was no strength or power in the new nature. Finally we hear him crying out, "O wretched man that I am! who shall deliver me from the body of this death?" (Rom. 7:24). Then something happened, and in verse 25 he says, "I thank God through Jesus Christ our Lord. . . ." It is through Him that you will have to do all your thanking, because that is where your help is going to come—through Him. ". . . So then with the mind I myself serve the law of God; but with the flesh the law of sin" (Rom. 7:25). That is the way that it is with all of us. We have that old nature, and it cannot do anything that will please God. In fact, Paul went on to say that it was against God.

"Because the carnal mind is enmity against God: for it is not subject to the law of God, neither indeed can be. So then they that are in the flesh cannot please God" (Rom. 8:7–8). We cannot please God in the flesh. Finally, Paul found victory by yielding to the Spirit of God. What the law could not do, the Spirit now is able to do in our lives. How does one do it? It is not until you and I yield to Him that we can please Him. Yield means that it is an act of the will of a regenerated person submitting himself to the will of God. And that is exactly what Jacob did. Jacob won, but he got the victory, not by fighting and struggling, but by yielding. What a picture we have here in him, and we are told that all these things happened unto them as examples to us (see 1 Cor. 10:11).

CHAPTER 33

THEME: Jacob meets Esau; Jacob journeys to Shalem

In the previous chapter we saw the high point in the life of Jacob, which was his encounter with God. On that night "a man" wrestled with him, and the "man," not Jacob, did the wrestling. Jacob was not looking for another fight. He has Uncle Laban in back of him and Brother Esau ahead of him, and the last time he saw both of them they were breathing out threatenings against him. This man Jacob is not in a position to take on someone else. Therefore, the "man" took the initiative; He was the aggressor. He was, as we have seen, the preincarnate Christ. Jacob resisted Him until the touch of God crippled him. Then, recognizing at last who He was, Jacob clung to Him until He blessed him. From this point on we will begin to see a change in Jacob. As we follow his life in the chapter before us, we will think that we have met a new man. To tell the truth, he *is* a new man.

JACOB MEETS ESAU

And Jacob lifted up his eyes, and looked, and, behold, Esau came, and with him four hundred men. And he divided the children unto Leah, and unto Rachel, and unto the two handmaids [Gen. 33:1].

Jacob wants to spare his family; so he separates them from the others.

And he put the handmaids and their children foremost, and Leah and her children after, and Rachel and Joseph hindermost.

And he passed over before them, and bowed himself to the ground seven times, until he came near to his brother [Gen. 33:2–3].

I would love to have a picture of Jacob meeting his brother Esau! I suppose that while he was a mile away from him, he started bowing. He is coming with his hat in his hand because Esau has four hundred men with him, and Jacob doesn't know if he is coming as friend or foe.

> **And Esau ran to meet him, and embraced him, and fell on his neck, and kissed him: and they wept [Gen. 33:4].**

Well, they are twins, they are brothers. Let bygones be bygones. It looks as if God has certainly touched Esau's heart because he had sworn vengeance that he would kill Jacob.

> **And he lifted up his eyes, and saw the women and the children; and said, Who are those with thee? And he said, The children which God hath graciously given thy servant.**

> **Then the handmaidens came near, they and their children, and they bowed themselves.**

> **And Leah also with her children came near, and bowed themselves: and after came Joseph near and Rachel, and they bowed themselves [Gen. 33:5–7].**

Jacob introduces his family to his brother.

> **And he said, What meanest thou by all this drove which I met? And he said, These are to find grace in the sight of my lord [Gen. 33:8].**

Apparently Jacob believes for a moment that his strategy of approaching his brother has worked. But it wasn't necessary. Listen to Esau—what a change!

> **And Esau said, I have enough, my brother; keep that thou hast unto thyself [Gen. 33:9].**

Esau is saying, "You didn't need to send that to me. I have plenty already."

And Jacob said, Nay, I pray thee, if now I have found grace in thy sight, then receive my present at my hand: for therefore I have seen thy face, as though I had seen the face of God, and thou wast pleased with me.

Take, I pray thee, my blessing that is brought to thee; because God hath dealt graciously with me, and because I have enough. And he urged him, and he took it [Gen. 33:10–11].

This is almost a humorous scene. Up to this time, each was trying to get something from the other. This was especially true of Jacob. Now we find Jacob in a new role altogether. Here he is insisting that his brother take a gift. Esau says, "You don't have to give it to me. I have plenty." But Jacob *insists* that he accept it. Believe me, something has happened to Jacob!

He reminds me of Zacchaeus in the New Testament. When our Lord called him down and went with him into his house, something happened to Zacchaeus. He wasn't the same man that climbed up into the tree. He said he would no longer be the tax collector who had been stealing from people and had been dishonest. He wanted to return, not only anything that he had taken in a wrong way, but he wanted to restore it fourfold. What a change had taken place! You could certainly tell which house Jesus had visited.

Certainly there is a change that has taken place in Jacob. Before he had traded a bowl of stew to get a birthright; now he is willing to give flocks and herds to his brother for nothing! In fact, Jacob *insists* that he take them. Esau finally accepted the gift. In that day and in that land if one refused to take a gift which was urged upon him, it was considered an insult. Therefore, Esau takes the gift.

And he said, Let us take our journey, and let us go, and I will go before thee [Gen. 33:12].

Esau is saying, "N. w as you return to the land, let me go before you, show you the way, and be a protection for you."

> **And he said unto him. My lord knoweth that the children are tender, and the flocks and herds with young are with me: and if men should overdrive them one day, all the flock will die [Gen. 33:13].**

Jacob says, "I'm moving my family, and we have little ones, also we have young among the flocks and herds. We can't go very fast. You, of course, with that army of four hundred will probably want to move much faster; so you go ahead."

> **Let my lord, I pray thee, pass over before his servant: and I will lead on softly, according as the cattle that goeth before me and the children be able to endure, until I come unto my lord unto Seir [Gen. 33:14].**

Jacob says, "I can't keep up with you, Brother Esau. I'll just have to set my own pace. You go on ahead."

> **And Esau said, Let me now leave with thee some of the folk that are with me. And he said, What needeth it? let me find grace in the sight of my lord.**

> **So Esau returned that day on his way unto Seir [Gen. 33:15–16].**

Esau lived in southern Canaan in Seir, the "land of Edom," at thi. time. After their father's death, he moved to Mount Seir which God subsequently gave to Esau for a possession [Deut 2·5]

JACOB JOURNEYS TO SHALEM

> **And Jacob journeyed to Succoth, and built him an house, and made booths for his cattle: therefore the name of the place is called Succoth [Gen. 33:17]**

Now let us not pass by so quickly and easily here that we do not pay attention to what has happened. A great change has come over this man Jacob. You see, all of Jacob's clever scheming to present a gift to his brother Esau has just come to naught. God had prepared the heart of Laban not to harm Jacob, and God had prepared the heart of Esau to receive Jacob. Now he has peace on both fronts. Esau did not want the gift of Jacob because Esau himself had an abundance. When Jacob insisted, he took the gift out of courtesy. Both these brothers seem to be generous and genuine in their reconciliation. We have no reason to doubt it. Since Esau is now prosperous, and since he attached no particular value to his birthright anyway, there is no reason why he should not be reconciled to his twin brother.

Now the sunshine is beginning to fall on Jacob's life. Laban is appeased and Esau is reconciled. God had arranged all of this for him. Had Jacob been left to his own cupidity and his own cleverness, he would have come to his death in a violent manner. Before too long Jacob is going to look back over his life, and when he does, he is going to see the hand of God in his life, and he is going to give God the glory. However, the evil that he has sown is yet to bring forth a full harvest. Trouble is in the offing for this man. It is there waiting for him.

Esau rides off to Seir, and we bid good-bye to him for the time being. He will be back, however, for the funeral of his father Isaac, as we will see in chapter 35.

And Jacob came to Shalem, a city of Shechem, which is in the land of Canaan, when he came from Padan-aram; and pitched his tent before the city.

And he bought a parcel of a field, where he had spread his tent, at the hand of the children of Hamor, Shechem's father, for an hundred pieces of money [Gen. 33:18–19].

Jacob is sometimes criticized because he stopped here at Succoth and at Shalem and did not proceed on to Bethel. Actually, we ought not to expect too much of Jacob at this time. He's been crippled, and he is just learning to walk with his spiritual legs.

And he erected there an altar, and called it El-elohe-Israel [Gen. 33:20].

Jacob builds an altar here, just as his grandfather Abraham was accustomed to building altars wherever he went. The fine feature is that Jacob identifies his new name with the name of God. He calls it El-elohe-Israel which means, "God, the God of Israel." This indicates real growth in a man who is just learning to walk. Let's put it like this. This man is on the way to Bethel, but he hasn't arrived there yet. First he journeys to Succoth.

BIBLIOGRAPHY
(Recommended for Further Study)

Barnhouse, Donald Grey. *Genesis: A Devotional Exposition.* Grand Rapids, Michigan: Zondervan Publishing House, 1973.

Borland, James A. *Christ in the Old Testament.* Chicago, Illinois: Moody Press, 1978.

Davis, John J. *Paradise to Prison: Studies in Genesis.* Grand Rapids, Michigan: Baker Book House, 1975.

De Haan, M. R. *Genesis and Evolution.* Grand Rapids, Michigan: Zondervan Publishing House, 1962.

De Haan, M. R. *The Days of Noah.* Grand Rapids, Michigan: Zondervan Publishing House, 1962.

Gispen, William Hendrik. *Genesis.* Grand Rapids, Michigan: Zondervan Publishing House, 1982.

Jensen, Irving L. *Genesis—A Self-Study Guide.* Chicago, Illinois: Moody Press, 1967.

Kidner, Derek. *Genesis.* Downers Grove, Illinois: InterVarsity Press, 1967

Mackintosh, C. H. *Genesis to Deuteronomy.* Neptune, New Jersey: Loizeaux Brothers, 1972.

Meyer, F. B. *Abraham: The Obedience of Faith.* Fort Washington, Pennsylvania: Christian Literature Crusade, n.d.

Meyer, F. B. *Israel: A Prince With God.* Fort Washington, Pennsylvania: Christian Literature Crusade, n.d.

Meyer, F. B. *Joseph: Beloved—Hated—Exalted.* Fort Washington, Pennsylvania: Christian Literature Crusade, n.d.

Morgan, G. Campbell. *The Unfolding Message of the Bible*. Old Tappan, New Jersey: Fleming H. Revell Company, n.d.

Morris, Henry M. *The Genesis Record: A Scientific and Devotional Commentary*. Grand Rapids, Michigan: Baker Book House, 1976.

Morris, Henry M. and Whitcomb, John C., Jr. *The Genesis Flood*. Grand Rapids, Michigan: Baker Book House, 1961.

Pink, Arthur W. *Gleanings in Genesis*. Chicago, Illinois: Moody Press, 1922.

Stigers, Harold. *A Commentary on Genesis*. Grand Rapids, Michigan: Zondervan Publishing House, 1975.

Thomas, W. H. Griffith. *Genesis: A Devotional Commentary*. Grand Rapids, Michigan: Eerdmans Publishing Company, 1946.

Unger, Merrill F. *Unger's Commentary on the Old Testament*. Vol. 1. Chicago, Illinois: Moody Press, 1980.

Vos, Howard F. *Genesis*. Chicago, Illinois: Moody Press, 1975.

Wood, Leon J. *Genesis: A Study Guide Commentary*. Grand Rapids, Michigan: Zondervan Publishing House, 1975.

For additional material on creation, the Flood, and science, write to:

Institute for Creation Research
P.O. Box 2667
El Cajon, California 92021